GOOD SOUP

JORIS BIJDENDIJK & SAMUEL LEVIE

SNERT
JORIS BIJDENDIJK
BRANDT & LEVIE
SNERT
BRANDT & LEVIE × JORIS BIJDENDIJK

GOOD SOUP
52 COLORFUL RECIPES
FOR YEAR-ROUND COMFORT

JORIS BIJDENDIJK & SAMUEL LEVIE

T tra.publishing

PREFACE

Harira and spicy peanut soup from Africa, Indonesian rawon soup and Malaysian laksa from Asia, gazpacho and fish soups from around the Mediterranean—soup is so diverse and enjoyed by so many that every culture has its own. We both have many cherished memories in which soup was front and center. When we were children, sick and lying on the couch, our grandmother put a fragrant bowl of broth down in front of us. Soup was often served at parties, as well, because it's so deliciously simple, and after a cold day of family ice skating, when it would be accompanied by rye bread with a thick layer of butter and bacon. The first time we made fish stock as young cooks, it felt magical that we could produce something so insanely wonderful with only bones and shrimp heads.

In recent years, our shared love of soup took on outrageous proportions. Apart from making this colorful cookbook, we also participated in a giant traditional Freedom Dinner on the occasion of the Dutch national holiday Freedom Day, celebrated on May 5. We cooked Pumpkin Soup with Ginger and Coconut (page 56) for a whopping ten thousand people and launched our business, SNERT, with Dutch Split Pea Soup (page 102) and three other canned soups. Sharing our love for soup proved contagious. Inspirational stories came our way from all over. We heard about people traveling the world to eat one particular crab soup at a market in Bangkok and watched the fantastic movie *Tampopo* about a Japanese woman searching for the perfect ramen recipe. This book is an ode to soup in all its manifestations. We share fifty-two recipes of our favorite soups with you. Not one week of the year will have to go by without a tasty bowl.

Samuel & Joris

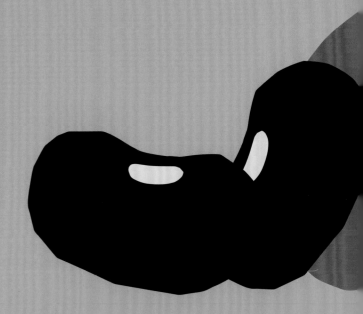

ALL RECIPES ARE INTENDED FOR 4 TO 6 PEOPLE UNLESS OTHERWISE SPECIFIED.

YELLOW GAZPACHO 52

PUMPKIN SOUP WITH GINGER AND COCONUT 56

LENTIL AND PUMPKIN SOUP 58

CARROT AND CORIANDER SOUP 60

SWEET POTATO SOUP WITH CASSAVA AND PLANTAIN 62

SWEET-AND-SOUR SHELLS WITH TURMERIC 64

PEACH SOUP WITH BURRATA 66

SHRIMP BISQUE 68

TOMATO CREAM SOUP WITH SAUSAGE OR MEATBALLS 72

GOULASH WITH BELL PEPPERS 74

NORTH SEA FISH SOUP 76

HARIRA 80

NOODLES IN BEEF BROTH 82

ZUPPA DI BACCALÀ 84

RED CABBAGE SOUP WITH RICOTTA DUMPLINGS 88

COLD BEET SOUP WITH PURPLE BASIL AND BLACKBERRIES 90

ROASTED VITELOTTE POTATO SOUP WITH GOAT CHEESE 92

BORSCHT 94

PURPLE SWEET POTATO SOUP 96

GREEN GAZPACHO WITH BURRATA 100

DUTCH SPLIT PEA SOUP 102

GREEN ASPARAGUS AND PEA SOUP WITH A SALAD OF HARICOTS VERTS AND ALMONDS 104

ZUCCHINI AND BREAD SOUP 106

GREEN CURRY SOUP WITH BROCCOLI 108

CALDO VERDE WITH CHORIZO 110

WATERCRESS SOUP 112

SOUP TYPES

Soups can quite naturally be divided into four main types.

CLEAR AND LIGHT SOUPS have stock or vegetable juice as a base. Therefore, the broths of these soups deserve full attention. In a good clear soup, what floats in the broth should not be too abundant and should be subtle and cooked in such a way that it retains its own texture. The individual ingredients remain recognizable. Think of Chicken Soup, for instance (page 120). But you can also use vegetable juice to make a clear or light soup, such as Cold Beet Soup with Purple Basil and Blackberries (page 90).

Then we come to **HEARTY SOUPS,** also known as main-dish soups. Dutch Split Pea Soup is a prime example of this type of soup (page 120), as are Borscht (page 94), Surinamese Brown Bean Soup (page 124), and Rawon Soup with Green Onions and Bean Sprouts (page 144). These thick soups are filled with rich ingredients and provide interesting new flavors through combinations of their elements. Not all ingredients can be identified individually when tasting these soups, but we believe that this is less important than the overall experience.

The texture of **CREAMY SOUPS** makes them feel velvety in the mouth. The tongue gets a light coating that allows for a powerful tasting experience. Soups can be thickened with flour or another binding agent, but there are many ways to achieve the effect. In French cuisine, a roux is used—a mixture of flour and butter—to thicken soup. We use a roux in the White Asparagus Soup with Tarragon Dressing (page 32). Then again, in Moroccan cuisine, there is tadouira, a mixture of flour and water, sometimes supplemented with tomato paste and coriander, which thickens Harira (page 80), for example. Soup can also be thickened with dairy or a plant-based milk, making it nice and creamy. Think of a generous knob of butter in North Sea Fish Soup (page 76), cream in Tomato Cream Soup with Sausage or Meatballs (page 72), or coconut milk in Thai Coconut Soup (page 28).

And last but not least: **PUREED SOUPS**. These soups can be the perfect way to use leftovers. If you make a tasty Pumpkin Soup with Ginger and Coconut (page 56), you can also empty the crisper drawer of your fridge. You boil everything in one go and then stick it in the immersion blender. As tasty and easy as you like! Pureed soups can also be made from raw ingredients and are deliciously fresh, like Ajo Blanco (White Gazpacho) with Grapes and Toasted Almonds (page 26) or Green Gazpacho with Burrata (page 100).

FLAVORINGS AND TOPPINGS

We love making our own stocks. And we usually don't use a set recipe for them. If we have chicken for our family dinner, we use the carcass for chicken stock. Do you have some vegetable scraps left over? Use them for stock! When we buy fish at the market, we save the bones and heads for stock. Shrimp or crab shells? Stock. Our freezers are filled with all kinds of containers and bags that we keep on hand for soup. Are you insecure about your stock skills? You'll find some easy recipes in the Basic Stocks section on pages 20-21. But feel free to deviate from these recipes and get creative.

You can also make an excellent soup without stock. There are a number of flavorings that can help give the soup depth on those occasions when you don't have stock available. Here are some of our favorites.

BOUILLON CUBES

You can be as dismissive as you like about them, and to be honest, we'd prefer to turn down a cup of chicken broth made from a bouillon cube. Still, using a bouillon cube is just fine to add depth to some soups. We always prefer homemade stock, but we also have our bouillon cubes on hand.

MISO

Fermented soybean paste. A magical Japanese substance that provides deep, nutty flavors. You know it from miso soup, of course, but a tablespoon of miso in a vegetable soup is definitely not out of place. We make our own miso from a variety of legumes and grains and recommend that you always have miso on hand.

DASHI

A Japanese flavoring based on bonito flakes (dried, fermented, and smoked shavings of skipjack tuna), mushrooms (usually dried shiitakes), and seaweed (kombu, to be exact). Incredibly tasty thanks to the different sources of umami. You can prepare the dashi stock yourself by combining the aforementioned individual ingredients (see page 22), but there are also instant varieties available in powdered or concentrated form. Sometimes you're allowed to cheat a little!

MARMITE

Something that English people put on their toast, marmite is a yeast extract-based spread that has a similar effect to stock. It's like taking a high-speed train to flavorville and creates real depth. It's perfect for those who want to keep their mushroom soup vegetarian but still add a bit of "meatiness" to the body of a soup.

FISH SAUCE

While fish sauce is widely used in Southeast Asia, Europe also has its own fish sauce: garum. This was already in use back in the time of the Roman Empire. It's a by-product of pickled fish and brightens up your fish soup or laksa significantly.

TOPPINGS

Soup is soup. It can be delicious on its own, but you can really turn it into something exciting by adding your choice of topping. We have added a separate topping for almost every soup in this book. The toppings add contrast in flavor and texture and make a real visual difference. Presentation is the first element of any meal. Toppings can be totally varied: roasted nuts, fresh herbs, vegetables, or a lovely crusty bread are all good. Thinly sliced fennel seasoned with lemon gives a heavier soup like the Cuttlefish Soup with Crostini and Fennel Salad (page 138) a fresh component. A soup that might otherwise be quite monotonous suddenly becomes exciting. We love crisped bits of bread, also known as croutons. A sustainable way to use up old bread, croutons go with almost any soup.

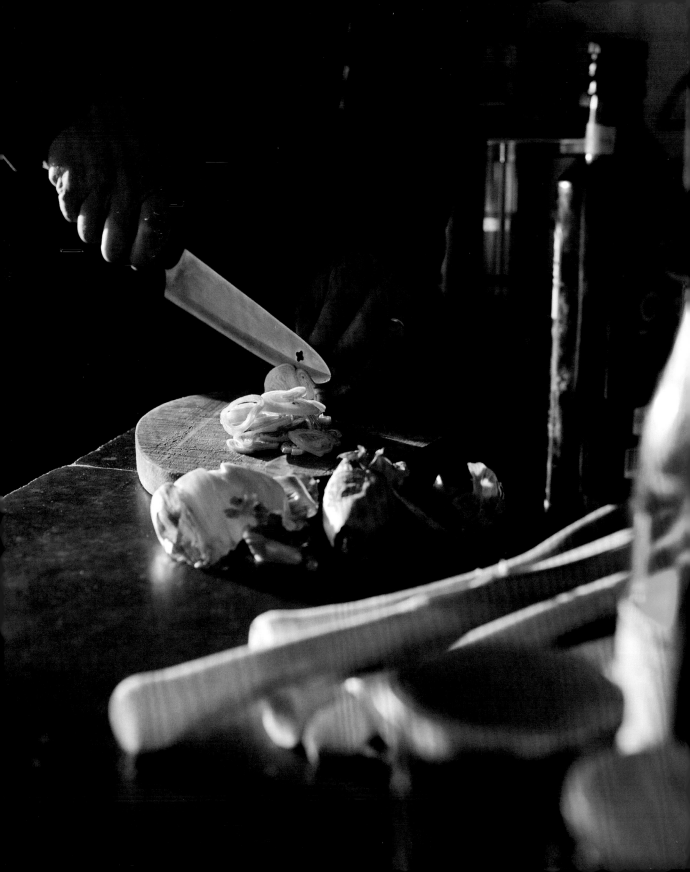

BASIC STOCKS

Making your own stock is easy and essential for preparing really good soup. It deepens the flavors. When using only water, a soup often remains quite flat. There are, of course, many shortcuts available that can be used to flavor soup just as well, such as ready-made stocks or bouillon cubes. You can always opt for that, of course, and it's a lot faster, but it can also get pricey and often these can contain a lot of additives that you don't necessarily want in your soup. Making your own stock results in a healthier product, is a lot cheaper and tastier, and is also fun to do.

Below are seven basic recipes. Recipes that are relatively quick to prepare yield about 1 ½ quarts of stock: the dashi, vegetable, mushroom, fish, and seafood stocks. For recipes that take more than 2 hours, the yield is about 4 quarts. After all, if you have the pan on the fire for all that time, you want to get more soup out of it, too. Stock is ideal for freezing in plastic containers or bags and will keep for about 6 months in the freezer. Make sure to mark each container or bag with the date and contents.

VEGETABLE STOCK
1 LARGE LEEK, FINELY DICED
2 CELERY RIBS, FINELY DICED
1 ONION, FINELY DICED
2 CARROTS, FINELY DICED
½ CUP SUNFLOWER OIL
½ BUNCH OF FLAT-LEAF PARSLEY
2 SPRIGS OF THYME
5 LOVAGE LEAVES
1 BAY LEAF
1 SPRIG OF ROSEMARY
5 BLACK PEPPERCORNS

Sauté the leek, celery, onion, and carrots in the sunflower oil in a soup pan. Add 8 cups of water and the remaining ingredients and bring to a boil. Turn the heat to low and cook for 20 minutes. Strain the stock and discard what remains in the strainer.

CHICKEN STOCK
2 SHALLOTS, FINELY DICED
1 LEEK, FINELY DICED
2 CELERY RIBS, FINELY DICED
5½ POUNDS CHICKEN (WING, BACK, NECK, CARCASS), IN PIECES
3 SPRIGS OF THYME
4 BAY LEAVES
½ GARLIC BULB
1 SMALL HANDFUL OF CELERY LEAVES

Combine the diced vegetables in a pan with 4 quarts of water. Add the chicken, thyme, bay leaves, garlic, and celery leaves and slowly bring to a boil. Regularly skim off any impurities that bubble to the surface with a slotted spoon. Allow the stock to simmer just below boiling point for 4 hours. If you have a kitchen thermometer, aim for 200°F. Strain the stock first through a strainer and then through a cheesecloth. Discard what remains in the strainer and cloth (possibly incorporate the chicken meat into another dish). Let the stock cool in the refrigerator, then carefully remove the layer of solidified fat with paper towels.

FISH STOCK
1½ POUNDS WHITEFISH BONES AND HEADS
1 ONION, QUARTERED
2 CELERY RIBS, COARSELY CHOPPED
1 CARROT, SLICED
STRIPS OF ZEST FROM ½ ORGANIC LEMON
1 BAY LEAF
¼ BUNCH OF FLAT-LEAF PARSLEY
6 BLACK PEPPERCORNS
⅔ CUP WHITE WINE

Rinse the bones and heads well. Combine all the ingredients in a pan with 6 ⅓ cups of water and bring to a boil. Let boil for a few minutes, then lower the heat to allow the stock to simmer just below boiling point for 20 minutes. If you have a kitchen thermometer, aim for 200°F. With a slotted spoon, regularly skim off impurities that bubble to the surface. Strain the stock through a fine strainer. Discard what remains in the strainer. Use the fish stock within 2 days or freeze it for a later use.

21

SHELLFISH STOCK

1 POUND SHELLS AND HEADS OF SHRIMP, LOBSTER, OR CRAB
2 TBSP. SUNFLOWER OIL
1 ONION, GRATED
2 CLOVES GARLIC
½ FENNEL BULB, FINELY CHOPPED
1 TBSP. TOMATO PASTE
⅔ CUP WHITE WINE
1 BAY LEAF
5 BLACK PEPPERCORNS
3 TBSP. COGNAC OR RICARD (OPTIONAL)

Rinse the shells and heads well. Fry the shells and heads in the sunflower oil in a large pan. Add the onion, garlic, fennel, and tomato paste. Deglaze with white wine and pour in 6 ½ cups of water. Add the bay leaf and peppercorns. Cognac and Ricard are tasty flavorings, so add one if you like. Allow the stock to simmer for 20 minutes just below the boiling point. If you have a kitchen thermometer, aim for 200°F. Impurities will bubble to the surface; skim them off regularly with a slotted spoon. Strain the stock through a fine strainer. Discard what remains in the strainer. Use the shellfish stock within 2 days or freeze it for a later use. You can also make a more Asian shellfish stock by replacing the fennel and bay leaf with makrut lime leaf and lemongrass.

DASHI

1 ¾ OUNCES DRIED KOMBU SHEETS
¼ CUP SZECHUAN PEPPER
1½ CUPS DRIED SHIITAKE MUSHROOMS
2 CUPS DRIED BONITO FLAKES
5 TBSP. SOY SAUCE, PLUS MORE AS NEEDED
1½ TBSP. YUZU JUICE
SUGAR (OPTIONAL)
SAKE (OPTIONAL)
CHOPPED VEGETABLES (OPTIONAL)

Put the kombu sheets, Szechuan pepper, and shiitake mushrooms in a large saucepan with 2 quarts of water over low heat. Allow the flavors to infuse into the water by leaving it on the stove at 140°F for 1 hour. Strain the stock and return it into the pan. Discard what remains in the strainer. Heat the stock to about 175°F. Add the bonito flakes and allow them to infuse the water with their flavor for 1 minute, no longer! Scoop out the bonito flakes with a slotted spoon. Remove the pan from the heat and add the soy sauce and yuzu juice. If necessary, season further with sugar, sake, soy sauce, or chopped vegetables–however you like it best.

MEAT STOCK

2¼ POUNDS OXTAIL, CUT INTO 2-INCH PIECES
2¼ POUNDS OXTAIL, VEAL, BEEF, OR LAMB BONES (SHANK, LEG, NECK), CUT INTO 2-INCH PIECES
2 ONIONS, HALVED (DO NOT PEEL)
2 CARROTS, COARSELY CHOPPED
1 LEEK, COARSELY CHOPPED
2 CELERY RIBS, COARSELY CHOPPED
¼ CELERIAC, PEELED AND COARSELY CHOPPED
2 CUPS RED WINE
2 SPRIGS OF THYME
2 BAY LEAVES
½ GARLIC BULB
1 SMALL HANDFUL OF CELERY LEAVES

Preheat the oven to 450°F. Put the oxtail and bones in a roasting pan and place in the oven. Stir occasionally. After 10 minutes, add the onion, carrots, leeks, celery, and celeriac and roast for 20 to 30 minutes, stirring frequently, until the bones are nicely browned. Transfer everything to a large soup pot. With some water, deglaze the roasting pan by scraping up the browned bits (fond) and add to the soup pot. Top up the pan with 5 quarts of water. Bring to a boil. Impurities will bubble to the surface; skim them off regularly with a slotted spoon. Add the remaining ingredients. Cover and allow the soup to simmer for 6 to 8 hours just below boiling point. If you have a kitchen thermometer, aim for 200°F. Strain the stock first through a strainer and then through a cheesecloth. Discard the solids. Let the stock cool in the refrigerator, then carefully remove the layer of solidified fat with paper towels. Reduce the stock to the desired thickness.

MUSHROOM STOCK

10 OUNCES WHITE MUSHROOMS
7 OUNCES FRESH SHIITAKE MUSHROOMS
7 OUNCES ENOKI MUSHROOMS
2¼ OUNCES DRIED KOMBU SHEETS
⅔ CUP DASHI (OPTIONAL)

Chop the white mushrooms and shiitake mushrooms and put them in a pan. Cut off the bottom of the enokis and discard it; the top can be picked apart in the pan. Add water until everything is covered. Add the kombu and simmer for 20 minutes, then turn off the heat and let infuse for another 30 minutes. Strain the stock and boil to reduce gently until well flavored; add some dashi if necessary.

22

AJO BLANCO
(WHITE GAZPACHO) WITH GRAPES AND TOASTED ALMONDS

Combine the almonds in a blender with the vegetable stock and blend until you have a smooth mixture. This will take about 10 minutes. If you think your blender is overheating, run it in stages. Add the white bread and run the blender again until everything is smooth. Add the grapes, apples, garlic, and vinegars, and blend again until you have a velvety smooth soup.

Finally, add the olive oil in a thin stream while the blender is running on low to create a nice emulsion. If you do it too quickly there is a chance that the soup will separate. Strain the Ajo Blanco through a fine strainer. If necessary, push the last remaining soup through the sieve with the rounded side of a spoon. Chill the soup in the refrigerator for at least 2 hours.

For the topping, toast the almonds in a dry skillet until golden brown. Cut the grapes in halves lengthwise.

Serve the soup cold with the toasted almonds and grapes on top and a drizzle of olive oil.

* You may not need all the stock; start with 3 cups and watch the thickness of the soup. Add stock later if necessary.

4 CUPS BLANCHED SLICED ALMONDS
4 ½ CUPS VEGETABLE STOCK OR WATER*
8 SLICES STALE WHITE BREAD WITHOUT CRUST, IN PIECES
2 ⅔ CUPS SEEDLESS GREEN GRAPES
2 GREEN APPLES, PEELED, CORED, AND FINELY CHOPPED
6 CLOVES GARLIC, CRUSHED
⅔ CUP SHERRY VINEGAR
⅔ CUP RICE VINEGAR
¾ CUP OLIVE OIL

TOPPING
½ CUP SLICED BLANCHED ALMONDS, COARSELY CHOPPED
⅔ CUP SEEDLESS GREEN GRAPES
4 TO 6 TBSP. OLIVE OIL

THAI COCONUT SOUP

In large soup pan, heat the sunflower oil over medium-high heat. Add the onion, galangal, ginger, lemongrass, lime leaves, garlic, and tom yum paste. Sauté briefly and then deglaze the pan with 1 ¼ cups of water. Add the coconut milk, fish sauce, and palm sugar and bring to a boil. Be careful not to let the soup boil over. Remove the pan from the heat and add the lime juice. Season to taste with additional lime juice, palm sugar, or tom yum paste.

Allow the soup to cool and refrigerate overnight so that the flavors are well blended. The next day, strain the soup, discard the flavorings, and taste for seasoning.

Heat the soup, pour into bowls, and garnish with the paper-thin slices of raw mushroom, chili oil, green onions, and cilantro leaves.

1 TO 2 TBSP. SUNFLOWER OIL
1 LARGE ONION, GRATED
½ CUP PEELED AND COARSELY
  CHOPPED GALANGAL
½ CUP PEELED AND COARSELY
  CHOPPED FRESH GINGER
1 STALK OF LEMONGRASS,
  COARSELY CHOPPED
3 MAKRUT LIME LEAVES,
  VEINS REMOVED
2 CLOVES GARLIC, HALVED
1 ½ TBSP. TOM YUM PASTE,
  PLUS MORE AS NEEDED
4 ¼ CUPS COCONUT MILK
3 TBSP. THAI FISH SAUCE
1 ½ TBSP. PALM SUGAR
  (OR SUBSTITUTE BROWN SUGAR),
  PLUS MORE AS NEEDED
JUICE OF 1 LIME, PLUS
  MORE AS NEEDED

TOPPING
10 WHITE MUSHROOMS,
  SLICED WAFER THIN
4 TO 6 TSP. THAI CHILI OIL
3 GREEN ONIONS, THINLY SLICED
½ BUNCH OF CILANTRO, LEAVES ONLY

JERUSALEM ARTICHOKE AND HAZELNUT SOUP WITH WATERCRESS SALAD

Preheat the oven to 375°F. In a large pan, sauté the Jerusalem artichokes and onion in the sunflower oil until soft, but make sure they do not brown. Add the garlic and thyme and sauté until fragrant. Deglaze the pan with the vegetable stock and add the milk, cream, and peppercorns. Stir well and bring to a boil. Turn down the heat and cook for 20 minutes.

Meanwhile, to make the topping, cut 4 unpeeled Jerusalem artichokes into wedges and place on a baking sheet lined with parchment paper. Drizzle with a little olive oil and sprinkle with salt. Roast in the oven for 20 minutes, until the Jerusalem artichokes are golden-brown and tender. Shave the remaining unpeeled Jerusalem artichokes into raw slices.

Pour the soup into a blender and blend until smooth, or use an immersion blender. Then pour the soup through a fine strainer to make it completely smooth. If necessary, push the last remaining soup through the sieve with the rounded side of a spoon. Pour the soup back into the pan and add the butter and hazelnut oil. Stir until the butter is absorbed. Keep the soup warm over low heat.

Make the watercress salad by combining the 4 tablespoons of olive oil, watercress, hazelnut oil, and balsamic vinegar and mixing well. Season with a little salt to taste. Place the Jerusalem artichoke wedges in the center of deep plates and top with the hazelnuts, shaved Jerusalem artichoke, and watercress salad. Pour the soup around it.

1 ½ POUNDS JERUSALEM ARTICHOKES (SUNCHOKES), PEELED AND SLICED ⅜-IN. THICK
1 WHITE ONION, GRATED
2 TBSP. SUNFLOWER OIL
1 CLOVE GARLIC, FINELY CHOPPED
1 SPRIG OF THYME
2 CUPS VEGETABLE STOCK
2 CUPS WHOLE MILK
2 CUPS LIGHT CREAM
3 BLACK PEPPERCORNS
7 TBSP. BUTTER, DICED
2 ¼ TSP. HAZELNUT OIL

TOPPING
5 JERUSALEM ARTICHOKES, UNPEELED
4 TBSP. OLIVE OIL, PLUS MORE AS NEEDED
SALT
1 BUNCH OF WILD WATERCRESS (OR SUBSTITUTE GARDEN CRESS)
1 TBSP. HAZELNUT OIL
2 TBSP. BALSAMIC VINEGAR
¼ CUP HAZELNUTS, ROASTED AND COARSELY CHOPPED

WHITE ASPARAGUS SOUP
WITH TARRAGON DRESSING

Peel the asparagus with a peeler and cut off the ends. Leave 2 or 3 asparagus whole, cut the rest into pieces. Heat the vegetable stock in a large pan over medium-high heat. Add the peels and ends to the vegetable stock and cook for 10 minutes. Strain the flavorings from the stock and discard them.

In a skillet over medium-high heat, sauté the flour in the butter, making a roux while stirring. Pour in the stock and bring to a boil, stirring. Add the sliced asparagus and cook until almost tender. Add the milk and cream. When the asparagus are fully cooked, after approximately 15 minutes, transfer the soup to a blender and blend until smooth, or use an immersion blender. Keep warm over low heat.

To make the topping, put the tarragon leaves (keep a few for the garnish) in a mortar with the white wine vinegar and olive oil and grind into a smooth, green dressing. Using a peeler, shave the remaining whole asparagus into thin strips.

Divide the asparagus strips among the bowls and pour the hot soup on top. Finish with the tarragon dressing and reserved tarragon leaves and grate a small pinch of nutmeg over each bowl.

1 ¾ POUNDS WHITE ASPARAGUS
3 ⅓ CUPS VEGETABLE STOCK
3 TBSP. FLOUR
2 TBSP. BUTTER
¾ CUP WHOLE MILK
¾ CUP LIGHT CREAM

TOPPING
3 SPRIGS OF TARRAGON,
   JUST THE LEAVES
1 TBSP. WHITE WINE VINEGAR
1 TBSP. OLIVE OIL
WHOLE NUTMEG

FENNEL AND WHITE BEAN SOUP

Finely chop the fennel bulb and reserve some green fennel fronds for the topping. Sauté the fennel, shallot, potato, and dried chili in a large pan with the olive oil. Add the thyme and garlic, sauté briefly, then deglaze with the stock. Bring to a boil and simmer for a good 20 minutes. Rinse the cannellini beans under cold running water. Add to the pan and simmer for another 10 minutes. Blend the soup in a blender until it's smooth or use an immersion blender.

To finish, divide the soup among the bowls and garnish with some fennel fronds, wafer-thin sliced fennel, lemon zest, and a drizzle of olive oil.

10 OUNCES FENNEL BULB(S)
1 SHALLOT, FINELY CHOPPED
10 OUNCES POTATO, PEELED AND
  FINELY CHOPPED
1 DRIED CHILI
2 TBSP. OLIVE OIL
3 SPRIGS OF THYME
3 CLOVES GARLIC
6 ½ CUPS VEGETABLE STOCK
1 (14-OUNCE) CAN CANNELLINI BEANS,
  DRAINED

TOPPING
FENNEL FRONDS
½ FENNEL BULB, SLICED WAFER THIN
GRATED ZEST OF 1 ORGANIC LEMON
1 TBSP. OLIVE OIL

SUNFLOWER SEED AND CELERIAC SOUP WITH PARSNIP AND SAGE

This recipe is enough for about 8 servings, so either make it for a dinner party or freeze the extra. Make a cartouche by cutting out a circle of parchment paper that will fit on top of the soup pan. Make a small hole in the center for steam to escape. The cartouche keeps the ingredients from drying out. Heat the sunflower oil in a skillet over medium-high heat and toast the sunflower seeds in the oil. Add the onions and sauté for a few minutes. Add the cubed celeriac to the pan and pour in the apple juice. Cover with the cartouche and simmer gently for 1 hour; the apple juice will reduce slightly.

Remove the cartouche and pour 4 ¼ cups of water into the pan. Bring to a boil and simmer the soup gently until the celeriac is really well cooked and tender. Transfer to a blender or use an immersion blender to process the soup until nice and smooth. Season with the miso, a pinch of salt, and a pinch of cayenne.

To make the topping, heat the sunflower oil in a skillet over medium-high heat. Add the handful of sunflower seeds and toast until golden brown. Scoop the seeds out of the pan and add the parsnip. Sauté the parsnip pieces with salt and pepper until soft and tender. Add the sage to the pan and immediately place the parsnips and sage in the soup bowls. Pour the hot soup into the bowls and garnish with the chervil, shallot, and toasted sunflower seeds.

3 TBSP. SUNFLOWER OIL
¾ CUP SUNFLOWER SEED KERNELS
2 ONIONS, GRATED
1 ¾ POUNDS CELERIAC, PEELED AND CUT INTO SMALL CUBES
2 CUPS APPLE JUICE
2 TBSP. WHITE MISO
SALT
GROUND CAYENNE

TOPPING
1 TBSP. SUNFLOWER OIL
HANDFUL OF SUNFLOWER SEED KERNELS
1 PARSNIP, PEELED AND COARSELY CHOPPED
SALT AND FRESHLY GROUND BLACK PEPPER
8 LEAVES OF SAGE, CUT INTO THIN STRIPS
1 BUNCH OF CHERVIL, FINELY CHOPPED
1 SHALLOT, VERY FINELY CHOPPED

36

MUSSEL CHOWDER

Make the mussel stock first. Rinse the mussels under cold running water. Discard any mussels that are open. Sauté the mussels, while still in the shells, in sunflower oil over high heat in a tall pan. Add the vegetables and herbs and deglaze with the white wine. Reduce by half. Add 6 cups of water. Simmer gently for 20 minutes. Pour through a strainer and then reduce the stock until you are left with about 3 ¼ cups. The mussels left in the strainer can be used as additional garnish; you can discard the rest of the flavorings. Set aside.

In a pan with the sunflower oil, gently sauté the leeks, garlic, bay leaf, and thyme; do not let them brown. Add the potato and sauté for a moment. Deglaze the pan with the white wine. Reduce by half and add the mussel stock and saffron. Let the potato and leeks cook for about 15 minutes until tender. Remove the bay leaf and thyme. Add the cream and butter. Transfer the soup to a blender and process until smooth, or use an immersion blender. Keep warm over low heat.

To make the topping, blanch five mussels at a time in a pot of boiling water that's as salty as the sea. As soon as they open, immediately transfer them into ice water or hold them under ice-cold running water. Remove the mussels from the shell (or leave them in for added flair in presentation). Boil the onion, celery, celeriac, and potato in the same water until they're tender. Pour the soup into the bowls and garnish with the mussels, bacon bits and diced onion, celery, celeriac, potato, and a few drops of olive oil.

MUSSEL STOCK
- 2 ¼ POUNDS MUSSELS (RESERVE 15 FOR GARNISH)
- 1 TBSP. SUNFLOWER OIL
- 4 CELERY RIBS, COARSELY CHOPPED
- ¼ CELERIAC, PEELED AND COARSELY CHOPPED
- 1 WHITE ONION, COARSELY CHOPPED
- 2 CLOVES GARLIC
- 4 SPRIGS OF THYME
- 1 BAY LEAF
- 2 CUPS WHITE WINE

CHOWDER
- 1 TBSP. SUNFLOWER OIL
- 1 CUP SLICED LEEK, WHITE PART ONLY
- 1 CLOVE GARLIC
- 1 BAY LEAF
- 2 SPRIGS OF THYME
- 1 ⅓ CUPS DICED POTATO (⅜-IN. CUBES)
- 7 TBSP. WHITE WINE
- 3 ¼ CUPS REDUCED MUSSEL STOCK (SEE DIRECTIONS)
- A FEW THREADS OF SAFFRON
- ¾ CUP LIGHT CREAM
- 7 TBSP. BUTTER, DICED

TOPPING
- 15 RESERVED MUSSELS (WITH SHELL) FROM THE MUSSEL STOCK
- SALT
- 1 CUP COARSELY CHOPPED ONION
- 1 CUP DICED CELERY (⅜-IN. CUBES)
- 1 ½ CUPS DICED CELERIAC (⅜-1N. CUBES)
- 1 CUP DICED POTATO (⅜-IN. CUBES)
- 1 POUND BACON, COOKED, DRAINED, AND CRUMBLED
- 2 TBSP. OLIVE OIL

CORN AND JALAPEÑO SOUP

In a tall pan, sauté the onions and corn in sunflower oil over medium-high heat. Add the whole habanero, sauté for a moment, and then take it out of the pan. If you find habanero too spicy, substitute a less spicy chili. Deglaze with 4 cups of the vegetable stock and simmer for 20 minutes. Transfer the soup to a blender with the remaining 2 cups of the vegetable stock and the jalapeño liquid or use an immersion blender.

To make the topping, mix together the beans, corn, peas, bell pepper, and chili oil. Divide the soup among the bowls and garnish with the topping mix. Place the habanero in the soup for those who dare.

1 ½ ONIONS, GRATED
5 ½ CUPS DRAINED CANNED CORN
3 TBSP. SUNFLOWER OIL
1 HABANEROS
6 CUPS VEGETABLE STOCK
4 TBSP. JALAPEÑO JUICE (FROM JAR)

TOPPING
6 TBSP. DRAINED AND RINSED CANNED
   BLACK BEANS
⅔ CUP DRAINED CANNED CORN
¾ CUP FROZEN PEAS
⅔ CUP DICED RED BELL PEPPER
CHILI OIL, TO TASTE

LAKSA

Make the curry paste first. Combine the shallots, garlic, ginger, lemongrass, lime leaves, coriander seeds, turmeric, red chilis, and sunflower oil in a food processor. Process for about 5 minutes to form a smooth curry paste.

Peel the shrimp and save the shells and heads (if you have purchased shrimp with the heads on). Fry the shells and heads in a large pan with the sunflower oil. Pour the vegetable stock on top of this. Cook for 10 minutes and apply pressure to the shells and/or heads with a masher so that you get as much of the juices from the shrimp heads as possible. Pour the stock through a strainer. Discard what remains in the strainer. Return the pan to the heat with a splash of sunflower oil. Fry the curry paste until the oil separates from it. Deglaze the pan with the stock. Add the coconut milk and bring to a boil. Add the peeled shrimp and allow them to cook for 5 minutes. Season the soup with the fish sauce and sugar.

Cook the rice noodles until tender according to package directions. Divide the noodles among the bowls, topping with the green onions, bean sprouts, chili oil, and shrimp. Pour the hot soup over and garnish with the cilantro leaves. Cut 1 lime into wafer-thin slices and divide those among the bowls as well. Put half a lime next to each bowl, so that everyone can add as much acidity as they like.

CURRY PASTE
- 2/3 CUP FINELY CHOPPED SHALLOTS
- 3 CLOVES GARLIC
- 2 TBSP. PEELED AND FINELY CHOPPED FRESH GINGER
- 3 LEMONGRASS STALKS, INNER PART FINELY CHOPPED
- 4 MAKRUT LIME LEAVES, VEINS REMOVED
- 2 TSP. CORIANDER SEEDS
- 6 TBSP. PEELED AND GRATED TURMERIC ROOT, OR 2 TBSP. GROUND
- 2 FRESH RED CHILIS, SEEDED
- 5 TBSP. SUNFLOWER OIL

SOUP
- 12 OUNCES SHRIMP
- 2 TBSP. SUNFLOWER OIL, PLUS MORE AS NEEDED
- 5 CUPS VEGETABLE STOCK
- 1 2/3 CUPS COCONUT MILK
- 3 TBSP. THAI FISH SAUCE
- 1 1/2 TSP. SUGAR

TOPPING
- 7 OUNCES RICE NOODLES
- 2 GREEN ONIONS, THINLY SLICED
- 7 OUNCES MUNG BEAN SPROUTS
- CHILI OIL, TO TASTE
- 1/2 BUNCH OF CILANTRO, LEAVES ONLY
- 3 TO 4 LIMES

44

VICHYSSOISE

WITH POTATO CRUMBLE

Vichyssoise is traditionally eaten cold, but we like it warm, too. We use only the leek whites and save the greens for stock (see pages 21-22). Sauté the potatoes, leeks, thyme, preserved lemon, and the garlic in a large pan with the butter for a few minutes. Deglaze with the stock and add the milk. Cook for about 20 minutes, until the leeks and potatoes are tender. Remove the thyme and garlic. Transfer the hot soup to a blender and process until smooth, or use an immersion blender. Strain the soup through a fine strainer. If necessary, push the last remaining soup through the sieve with the rounded side of a spoon. Season with the horseradish and salt to taste.

To make the topping, cut the potato into $\frac{1}{8}$-inch cubes. Rinse the cubes under cold running water and then pat them dry with paper towels. In a deep pan, heat the sunflower oil to 375°F and deep-fry the potato cubes until golden brown. Scoop them out of the oil with a slotted spoon and put them on paper towels to drain. Sprinkle with salt and, at the last minute, mix the diced potatoes with the lemon zest and chives.

Divide the soup among the bowls and finish with the potato crumble and a sprinkling of pepper.

1 POUND POTATOES,
  PEELED AND CHOPPED
5 CUPS SLICED LEEKS
  (WHITE PART ONLY)
1 SPRIG OF THYME
1 PRESERVED LEMON (PULP ONLY; USE
  THE ZEST FOR THE CRUMB)
1 CLOVE GARLIC, LEFT WHOLE
3 ½ TBSP. BUTTER
4 ¼ CUPS CHICKEN OR
  VEGETABLE STOCK
1 CUP WHOLE MILK
2 TSP. GRATED HORSERADISH
  (FRESH OR FROM JAR), OR TO TASTE
SALT

TOPPING
1 LARGE POTATO (PREFERABLY
  YELLOW), PEELED
2 CUPS SUNFLOWER OIL
SALT
ZEST OF ½ PRESERVED LEMON,
  VERY FINELY MINCED
¼ BUNCH OF CHIVES, FINELY CHOPPED
  (OPTIONAL)
FRESHLY GROUND BLACK PEPPER

DAHL

In Indian cuisine, dahl is often combined with other dishes such as rice, flatbread, sautéed spinach, or mushrooms (also with spices added, of course).

To make the spiced oil, in a large pan, sauté the cumin and coriander along with the garlic, onion, garam masala, and turmeric in the sunflower oil. Add the tomato paste and sauté for a moment. Allow to cool.

Rinse the yellow split peas under cold running water and put them in a large saucepan with the vegetable stock or water. Bring to a boil, turn the heat down to low, and cook gently for about 1 hour. Grate the ginger and finely chop the green chili. Add to the pan and stir briskly with a whisk. You will see the split peas fall apart. Coarsely dice the tomatoes and finely chop the cilantro. Stir both into the dahl and remove the pan from the heat. Reserve ¼ cup of the cooled spice oil and stir the remainder into the dahl. Allow to settle for 10 minutes.

Cut the naan into small cubes and fry in a skillet with sunflower oil until crispy on all sides. Drain on paper towels. Finely chop the cilantro and mix in a bowl with the yogurt. Season to taste with salt and pepper.

Serve the dahl in bowls topped with the yogurt sauce, naan croutons, reserved spice oil, spinach, and lime juice.

SPICED OIL
1 TSP. GROUND CUMIN
1 ½ TSP. GROUND CORIANDER
3 CLOVES GARLIC, FINELY CHOPPED
1 ONION, GRATED
¾ TSP. GARAM MASALA
¾ TSP. GROUND TURMERIC
½ CUP SUNFLOWER OIL
2 TBSP. TOMATO PASTE

DAHL
1 CUP DRIED YELLOW SPLIT PEAS
4 ¼ CUPS VEGETABLE STOCK
   OR WATER
¾-IN. FRESH GINGER, PEELED
1 GREEN CHILI, SEEDED
2 TOMATOES
½ BUNCH OF CILANTRO

TOPPING
1 NAAN
1 TBSP. SUNFLOWER OIL
½ BUNCH OF CILANTRO
1 CUP PLAIN YOGURT
SALT AND FRESHLY GROUND
   BLACK PEPPER
HANDFUL OF YOUNG SPINACH LEAVES
JUICE OF 1 LIME

YELLOW PEA SOUP

Put the salt pork in a pan of cold water and cook for 40 minutes. Remove from heat and set aside. Meanwhile, wash the split peas in cold water.

Heat the sunflower oil over medium-high heat in a tall saucepan and add the shallots, celery, carrots, and garlic; sauté for a few minutes. Add the curry powder and turmeric and sauté briefly. Deglaze with the vegetable stock and add the coconut milk. Stir well and add the split peas, lemongrass, and lime leaves. Bring everything to a boil and let the soup simmer on low heat for 1 hour. Remove the lemongrass and lime leaves. The split peas fall apart when cooked. Dice the salt pork and mix three-quarters into the soup. Keep the rest for the garnish.

To make the topping, in a bowl, mix the red onion in red wine vinegar and massage well so that the onion bruises and absorbs the vinegar.

Pour the hot soup into bowls and garnish with the reserved salt pork, spicy peanuts, red onion, celery leaves, and some of the sambal oil to taste. Note that the katjang pedis (spicy peanuts) can be made from scratch by coating peanuts in egg whites, garlic powder, and flour and then deep frying them.

7 OUNCES SALT PORK
9 OUNCES YELLOW SPLIT PEAS
¼ CUP SUNFLOWER OIL
2 SHALLOTS, FINELY CHOPPED
2 CELERY RIBS, THINLY SLICED
2 CARROTS, DICED
3 CLOVES GARLIC, FINELY CHOPPED
2 TBSP. CURRY POWDER
1 TSP. GROUND TURMERIC
4 ¼ CUPS VEGETABLE STOCK
1 ⅔ CUPS COCONUT MILK
2 STALKS OF LEMONGRASS, BRUISED
3 MAKRUT LIME LEAVES

TOPPING
½ RED ONION, THINLY SLICED
2 TBSP. RED WINE VINEGAR
⅓ CUP KATJANG PEDIS (SPICY
   PEANUTS), COARSELY CHOPPED
10 CELERY LEAVES, FINELY CHOPPED
1 TBSP. SAMBAL, MIXED WITH
2 TBSP. SUNFLOWER OIL

YELLOW GAZPACHO

This recipe is enough for about eight bowls, so either make it for a dinner party or freeze the extra.

Toast the cumin seeds and turmeric in a dry pan over medium-high heat until fragrant. Transfer to a blender with tomatoes, cucumber, bell peppers, onion, mangoes, ginger, chilis, garlic, corn, pickled onions, vinegar, olive oil, and salt. Puree the soup until smooth and strain through a fine strainer over a pan.

Add the sprigs of mint, basil, and cilantro and bruise them a little, to release their flavors. Let the soup chill thoroughly in the refrigerator for at least 1 hour. Remove the herbs before serving.

To make the topping, toast the cumin seeds in a dry pan over medium-high heat until fragrant. Serve the soup topped with the toasted cumin seeds, slices of avocado, slices of cucumber, and a drizzle of green-herb oil.

1 TBSP. CUMIN SEEDS
1 TBSP. GROUND TURMERIC
3 LARGE PINEAPPLE TOMATOES
  (ABOUT 1 ¾ POUNDS)
1 CUCUMBER, PEELED
2 YELLOW BELL PEPPERS,
  STEMMED AND SEEDED
1 ONION, QUARTERED
2 RIPE MANGOES, PEELED
  AND PITTED
1 ½-IN. FRESH GINGER, PEELED
  AND SLICED

1 FRESH YELLOW CHILI, SEEDED
2 CLOVES GARLIC
KERNELS FROM 4 COOKED CORN COBS
  (OR 2 CUPS FROZEN
  CORN KERNELS, THAWED)
2 CUPS PICKLED PEARL ONIONS
1 CUP RICE VINEGAR
1 ⅔ CUPS OLIVE OIL
PINCH OF SALT
3 SPRIGS OF MINT
3 SPRIGS OF BASIL
3 SPRIGS OF CILANTRO

TOPPING
1 TBSP. CUMIN SEEDS
1 AVOCADO, PEELED, PITTED,
  HALVED, AND SLICED
1 CUCUMBER, THINLY SLICED
GREEN HERB OIL (SEE PAGE 96,
  OPTIONAL)

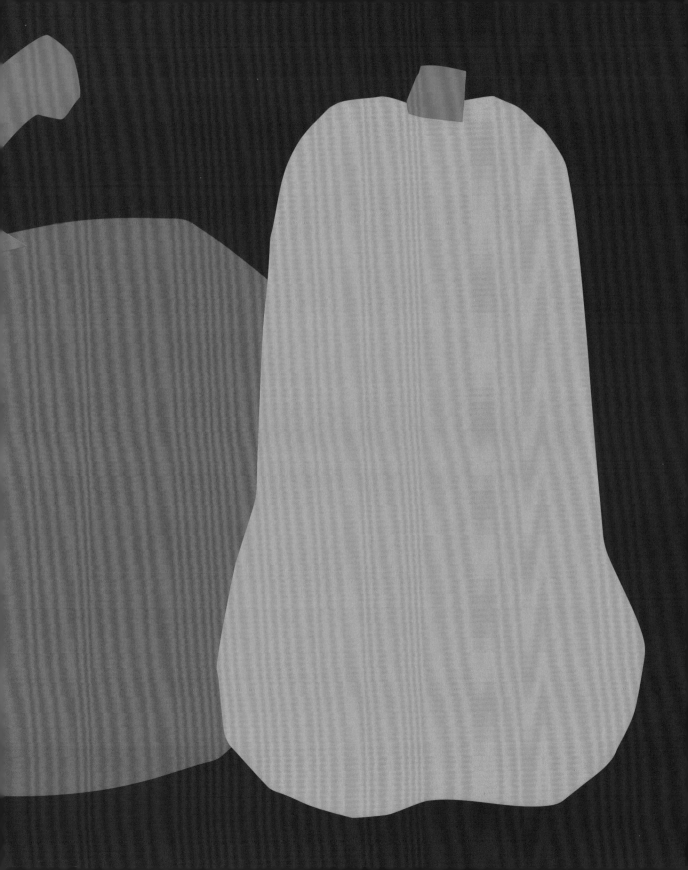

PUMPKIN SOUP

WITH GINGER AND COCONUT

Cut the pumpkin into small pieces. Sauté the onions in a large pan with the olive oil, cumin seeds, cayenne, garlic, and ginger. Add the pumpkin and sauté for 5 minutes without browning. Pour in the coconut cream and cook for about 30 minutes until everything is tender. If there is not enough liquid in the pan, a splash of water may be added. Blend the soup in a blender until it's smooth or use an immersion blender in the pan. Strain the soup. If necessary, push the last remaining soup through the sieve with the rounded side of a spoon. Season the soup with salt and pepper.

Serve the soup with a tablespoon of crème fraîche and toasted pumpkin seeds added to each bowl and a sprinkle of cumin seeds. Serve with breadsticks.

2 ¼ POUNDS PUMPKIN, PEELED, SEEDED, AND FIBERS REMOVED
2 ONIONS, GRATED
6 TBSP. OLIVE OIL
2 TBSP. CUMIN SEEDS
2 PINCHES OF GROUND CAYENNE
2 CLOVES GARLIC, CRUSHED
2 ½-IN. FRESH GINGER, PEELED AND FINELY CHOPPED
2 CUPS COCONUT CREAM
SALT AND FRESHLY GROUND BLACK PEPPER

TOPPING
4 TO 6 TBSP. CRÈME FRAÎCHE OR OLIVE OIL
4 TO 6 TBSP. PUMPKIN SEEDS, TOASTED
1 TBSP. CUMIN SEEDS, TOASTED
BREAD STICKS (OPTIONAL)

LENTIL AND PUMPKIN SOUP

Dip the tomatoes in hot water for a moment to loosen the skins. Remove the skins, then cut the flesh into coarse pieces. Toast the cumin seeds in a dry pan until fragrant. Sauté the onion and garlic in a large pan with the ghee. Add the curry masala, turmeric, cumin seeds, and cayenne and sauté briefly. Then add the tomato and sauté again for a moment. Add the lentils and pumpkin to the pan and stir everything well. After a few minutes, add the vegetable stock and cook for 25 minutes, until everything is tender. Pay close attention to which lentils you use, some are cooked after just a few minutes, others take longer. Adjust the cooking time accordingly. The pumpkin needs 20 to 30 minutes to cook through. Run the soup through a blender, making it as smooth or coarse as you like, or use an immersion blender. Season with salt to taste.

Serve the soup in bowls, top with the lime slices, lime juice, and lime zest, if using. Sprinkle with the Thai chilis.

2 TOMATOES
2 TSP. CUMIN SEEDS
1 ONION, GRATED
2 CLOVES GARLIC, CRUSHED
2 TBSP. GHEE OR SUNFLOWER OIL
3 HEAPING TSP. HIGH-QUALITY
  GARAM MASALA
1 TSP. GROUND TURMERIC

1 TSP. GROUND CAYENNE (OPTIONAL)
1 CUP RED LENTILS
14 OUNCES PUMPKIN FLESH
  (REMOVE SEEDS AND FIBERS),
  IN SMALL CUBES
6 CUPS VEGETABLE STOCK OR WATER
SALT

TOPPING
1 LIME, SLICED WAFER THIN
GRATED ZEST AND JUICE OF 2 MAKRUT
  LIMES (OPTIONAL)
3 GREEN AND/OR RED THAI CHILIS,
  SEEDED AND FINELY CHOPPED

CARROT AND CORIANDER SOUP

In a large pan, combine the leek, onion, celery, and carrots with the olive oil and sauté. Add the coriander. Pour in the vegetable stock, cover and cook everything for 15 minutes until the vegetables are tender. Transfer the soup to a blender and process until smooth, or use an immersion blender. Return the soup to the pan. Spoon the Greek yogurt into the soup and season with the chipotle hot sauce, salt, and pepper. Stir well.

To make the topping, cut the celery into cubes that are as small as possible and sauté in the olive oil for 2 minutes.

Spoon some Greek yogurt into each bowl, top with the celery and cilantro. Pour the hot soup around it and sprinkle with pepper.

1 LEEK, FINELY CHOPPED
1 ONION, FINELY CHOPPED
2 CELERY RIBS, FINELY CHOPPED
1 POUND CARROTS, FINELY CHOPPED
3 TBSP. OLIVE OIL
1 TBSP. GROUND CORIANDER
4 ¼ CUPS VEGETABLE STOCK
3 TBSP. GREEK YOGURT
1 TBSP. CHIPOTLE HOT SAUCE
   (OR MORE IF YOU LIKE THINGS SPICY,
   TO TASTE)
SALT AND FRESHLY GROUND
   BLACK PEPPER

TOPPING
1 CELERY RIB, THREADS REMOVED
1 TBSP. OLIVE OIL
4 TO 6 TBSP. GREEK YOGURT
½ BUNCH OF CILANTRO,
   FINELY CHOPPED
FRESHLY GROUND BLACK PEPPER

SWEET POTATO SOUP **WITH CASSAVA AND PLANTAIN**

Peel the sweet potatoes and cut into chunks. Sauté the sweet potatoes along with the onions in a large pan with the sunflower oil. Add 4 cups of the vegetable stock and cook for about 30 minutes, until the sweet potatoes are tender. Transfer to a blender along with the remaining 2 cups vegetable stock and puree until the soup is smooth or use an immersion blender. Finally, add the sour cream and give the soup a brief blitz. Keep warm over low heat.

For the topping, peel the sweet potato and cassava. Cut them into chunks. Cook in a large saucepan of water for 15 to 30 minutes, until tender. Drain everything. Peel the plantain, cut it lengthwise, then slice each half into slices about ¼ inch thick. In a pan, heat a generous layer of sunflower oil and deep fry the plantain slices until golden brown. Drain on paper towels and sprinkle with salt.

Pour the soup into bowls and garnish with the cooked cassava, sweet potato, fried plantain, cilantro leaves, coconut shreds, and lime juice.

1 ¾ POUNDS SWEET POTATO
2 ONIONS, GRATED
2 TBSP. SUNFLOWER OIL
6 CUPS VEGETABLE STOCK
½ CUP SOUR CREAM

TOPPING
14 OUNCES SWEET POTATO
10 ½ OUNCES CASSAVA
1 LARGE GREEN PLANTAIN
½ TO 1 CUP SUNFLOWER OIL
SALT
½ BUNCH OF CILANTRO,
  JUST THE LEAVES
HANDFUL OF COCONUT SHREDS
JUICE OF 1 LIME

SWEET-AND-SOUR SHELLS WITH TURMERIC

With a microplane, grate the garlic, ginger, and turmeric. Sauté these along with the lime leaves and lemongrass in a large pan with sunflower oil. Add the tomato paste and sauté for a moment. Add the fish stock and simmer for 20 minutes. Rinse the cockles under cold running water and discard those with broken shells. Put the cockles in the pan and put the lid on. Simmer for a few minutes so that all the shells open. Finely chop the red chili. Season the soup with the red chilis, fish sauce, sugar, and lime juice.

Serve the soup in bowls with a generous handful of green onions and cilantro in each bowl. Add a wedge of lime for those who like acidity.

* You can also make this recipe with mussels or clams.

3 CLOVES GARLIC
3 ½ OUNCES FRESH GINGER, PEELED
1 OUNCE TURMERIC ROOT, PEELED
2 MAKRUT LIME LEAVES,
  VEINS REMOVED
2 LEMONGRASS STALKS,
  THE INNER PART FINELY CHOPPED
3 TBSP. SUNFLOWER OIL
1 TBSP. TOMATO PASTE
3 ⅓ CUPS FISH STOCK
2 ¼ POUNDS COCKLES*
1 FRESH RED CHILI,
  (SEEDED IF DESIRED)
2 TBSP. THAI FISH SAUCE
1 TBSP. SUGAR
JUICE OF 1 LIME

TOPPING
3 GREEN ONIONS, THINLY SLICED
1 BUNCH OF CILANTRO,
  FINELY CHOPPED
1 LIME, CUT INTO 4 TO 6 WEDGES

PEACH SOUP WITH BURRATA

This recipe makes two to four small bowls. Serve it as an appetizer or double the recipe.

Set aside about one-quarter of the celery slices. Put the rest of the celery and the peaches, cucumber, garlic, and vinegar in a blender and blend until completely smooth. Season with a generous pinch of salt and refrigerate for at least 1 hour.

To make the topping, roast the red chili all around under the broiler or directly over the fire of a gas stove. The skin may blacken, and you can carefully peel that off when the pepper has cooled. Seed the chilis. Combine the chili with the salt and olive oil in the cup of a mini chopper or in a mortar and blend or crush into a red oil.

Serve the soup ice-cold topped with the burrata pieces, a drizzle of the smoky chili oil, the reserved celery, and a few tarragon leaves.

2 CELERY RIBS, THINLY SLICED
12 OUNCES RIPE PEACHES,
  PEELED AND DICED
  (FROZEN CAN ALSO BE USED)
½ CUCUMBER, PEELED AND DICED
1 CLOVE GARLIC
1 TBSP. RED WINE VINEGAR
SALT

TOPPING
1 FRESH RED CHILI
1 TSP. COARSE SALT
¼ CUP OLIVE OIL
1 BALL OF BURRATA,
  TORN INTO PIECES
2 TARRAGON SPRIGS, LEAVES ONLY

SHRIMP BISQUE

This recipe is enough for a bit more than four bowls, so either make it for a dinner party or freeze the extra.

Heat a large pan over medium-high heat and sauté the shrimp briskly in ¼ cup of the butter. Add the celery, fennel, leek, onion, garlic, bay leaf, and thyme and sauté for a few minutes. Add the tomatoes and tomato paste.

Flambé with the cognac by pouring the liquor into the pan and then igniting it. (Careful! Make sure your exhaust fan is off.) Simmer until the alcohol has evaporated, then do the same with the white wine. Pour water into the pan until the shrimp are just submerged. Stir in the orange juice, zest, and cayenne and simmer gently for 1 hour over low heat.

Strain the bisque through a clean cheesecloth over a saucepan and boil until you have about 20 percent left. Set the shrimp aside. The sauce should now have a strong and delicious taste. Using an immersion blender, blend in the remaining ½ cup of butter. Thick foam may float on the bisque. Pour out into deep plates or into coffee cups and garnish with a slice of bread, the sea lavender, peeled shrimp, possibly some green onion, and chili oil. Finish with a twist of pepper and serve the soup with the Gueuze beer.

4 ½ POUNDS SHRIMP,
  PEELED AND DEVEINED
¾ CUP (1 ½ STICKS) BUTTER, DICED
2 CELERY RIBS, THINLY SLICED
½ FENNEL BULB, FINELY CHOPPED
1 LEEK, THINLY SLICED
1 ONION, GRATED
2 CLOVES GARLIC, FINELY CHOPPED
1 BAY LEAF
1 SPRIG OF THYME
2 TOMATOES, FINELY CHOPPED
5 TBSP. TOMATO PASTE
¾ CUP COGNAC
1 ¾ CUPS WHITE WINE
GRATED ZEST AND JUICE OF
  1 ORGANIC ORANGE
1 TSP. GROUND CAYENNE

TOPPING
4 SLICES OF SOURDOUGH BREAD,
  TOASTED
1 ¾ OUNCE SEA LAVENDER
  (OPTIONAL)
1 GREEN ONION, THINLY SLICED
  (OPTIONAL)
FEW DROPS OF SMOKY CHILI OIL
  OR HARISSA OIL (SEE PAGES
  66 AND 96)
FRESHLY GROUND BLACK PEPPER
LAMBIC-STYLE GUEUZE BEER,
  TO SERVE (OPTIONAL)

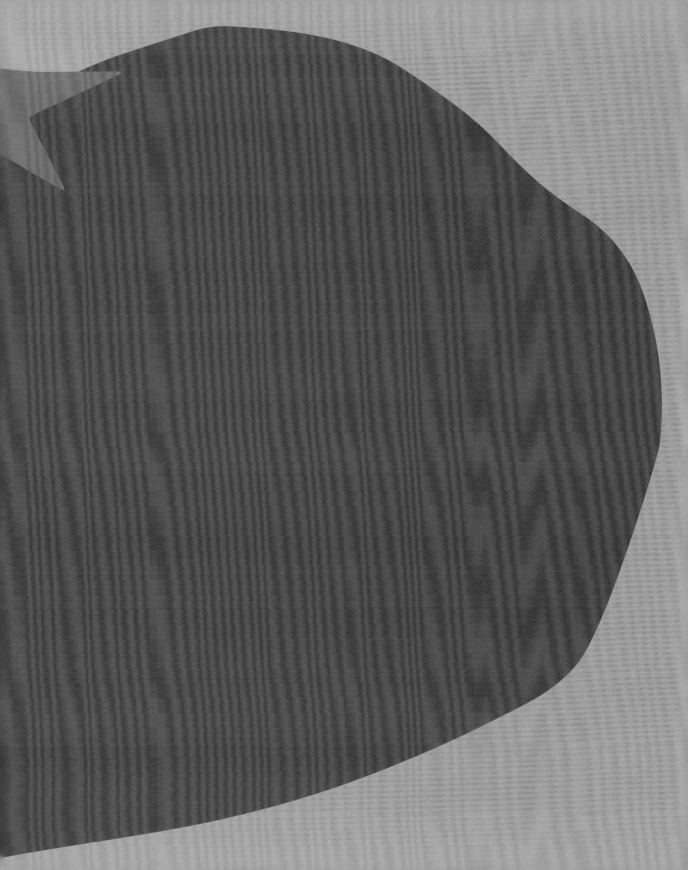

TOMATO CREAM SOUP WITH SAUSAGE OR MEATBALLS

In a large pan, sauté the onion and garlic in the olive oil. Add the tomato paste and sauté for 5 minutes. Then add the tomato puree, mushroom stock, fennel seeds, and dried porcini. Bring to a boil.

Remove the casing from the sausage and add the sausage meat (cut into pieces) to the stock. Or season the 50/50 beef and pork mixture with plenty of salt and pepper, lemon zest, and fennel seeds and add the breadcrumbs. Form the meat into balls and add to the stock.

Add the celeriac, cauliflower, fennel, beans, and celery to the stock in the pan and simmer for 15 minutes. Then stir in the cream. Season with salt and pepper to taste.

Pour the soup into bowls and garnish with the freshly grated Parmesan and basil.

1 SMALL ONION, GRATED
2 CLOVES GARLIC, FINELY CHOPPED
3 TBSP. EXTRA-VIRGIN OLIVE OIL
5 TBSP. TOMATO PASTE
1 ⅔ CUPS TOMATO PUREE
4 ¼ CUPS MUSHROOM STOCK
1 TSP. GROUND FENNEL SEEDS
  (PLUS MORE FOR THE MINCED MEAT,
  OPTIONAL)
1 TBSP. FINELY CHOPPED DRIED
  PORCINI MUSHROOMS
2 ITALIAN PORK SAUSAGES OR
  10 ½ OUNCES OF 50/50 GROUND
  BEEF AND PORK

SALT AND FRESHLY GROUND
  BLACK PEPPER
GRATED ZEST OF 1 ORGANIC LEMON
  (OPTIONAL)
½ CUP FRESH BREAD CRUMBS
  OR ¼ CUP DRIED (OPTIONAL)
½ CUP DICED CELERIAC
¾ CUP DICED CAULIFLOWER
1 CUP DICED FENNEL BULB
⅔ CUP CANNED FLAGEOLET BEANS
  (OR OTHER BEANS)
3 CELERY RIBS, FINELY CHOPPED
⅔ CUP LIGHT CREAM
  OR MASCARPONE

TOPPING
FRESHLY GRATED PARMESAN,
  FOR GARNISH
½ BUNCH OF BASIL,
  COARSELY CHOPPED

72

GOULASH WITH BELL PEPPERS

Pour the olive oil into a large soup pot or skillet and brown the meat all around. Add the bell peppers, chili, onions, and garlic and sauté. Then add the paprika, marjoram, caraway seeds, and bay leaf and sauté until the spices start to release their fragrance. Add the tomato paste and tomatoes to the pan and sauté for 1 minute. Deglaze with 1 cup of the beef stock and the red wine vinegar. Reduce by half. Then add enough of the remaining 3 ¼ cups stock to just cover the meat and simmer gently over low heat for 1 ½ to 2 hours, until tender. Add the potatoes to the goulash and cook for 15 minutes, until tender.

If necessary, you can add more stock (or water). Season the soup with salt and pepper.

Pour the soup into bowls and top each bowl with a tablespoon of sour cream.

---

2 TBSP. OLIVE OIL

1 POUND BONELESS BEEF SHORT RIBS, DICED INTO SMALL CUBES

2 RED BELL PEPPERS, SEEDED AND FINELY DICED

½ FRESH RED CHILI, SEEDED AND FINELY DICED

2 CUPS GRATED ONIONS

2 CLOVES GARLIC, CRUSHED

1 TBSP. SMOKED PAPRIKA

2 SPRIGS OF MARJORAM, LEAVES ONLY

1 ½ TSP. CARAWAY SEEDS

1 BAY LEAF

1 TBSP. TOMATO PASTE

2 TOMATOES, DICED

4 ¼ CUPS BEEF STOCK, PLUS MORE AS NEEDED

1 TBSP. RED WINE VINEGAR

1 ½ CUPS CUBED AND PEELED WAXY POTATOES (SUCH AS RED BLISS)

SALT AND FRESHLY GROUND BLACK PEPPER

TOPPING

4 TO 6 TBSP. SOUR CREAM

NORTH SEA FISH SOUP

Sauté the vegetables, herbs, and spices in a large pan with the sunflower oil. Add the tomato paste and sauté for a moment. Then place the fish on top of the vegetables in the pan. Deglaze with the Pernod and flambé by gently lighting the liquor with a lighter. Wait for the alcohol to burn up. Add the Noilly Prat and reduce everything by half. Halve the oranges, squeeze them over the pan, and add the squeezed halves to the pan as well. Add the fish stock and let everything cook very gently for about 1 hour or less. Remove the orange halves. Transfer the soup to a blender and process until smooth, or use an immersion blender. Strain the soup for extra smooth results and discard the remaining solids. Season with the colatura di alici, the orange juice and zest, pepper, and salt. Add the butter and stir until fully incorporated.

For the topping, sauté the spinach and garlic in the butter. Season with salt and pepper. Pour the soup into bowls and spoon the sautéed spinach into the center. Drizzle with the olive oil. If desired, serve another piece of poached fish in the soup.

1 LEEK, DICED
1 LARGE FENNEL BULB, DICED
2 SHALLOTS, DICED
2 CELERY RIBS, DICED
4 CLOVES GARLIC, MINCED
1 TBSP. FENNEL SEEDS
1 TBSP. CORIANDER SEEDS
2 TSP. FRESHLY GROUND BLACK PEPPER
1 FRESH RED CHILI
2 SPRIGS OF THYME
2 BAY LEAVES
4 PARSLEY STEMS
4 SPRIGS OF TARRAGON
4 SPRIGS OF BASIL
1 SMALL THREAD OF SAFFRON
2 TBSP. SUNFLOWER OIL
⅔ CUP TOMATO PASTE

3 ⅓ POUNDS WHITE-FLESH FISH FILETS, SUCH AS COD, BASS, GROUPER, HADDOCK, CATFISH, OR SNAPPER, IN 2-IN. PIECES
⅓ CUP PERNOD
1 ¼ CUPS NOILLY PRAT OR OTHER DRY VERMOUTH
2 ORGANIC ORANGES, PLUS GRATED ZEST AND JUICE OF 1
8 CUPS FISH STOCK
2 TBSP. ITALIAN FISH SAUCE (COLATURA DI ALICI, OR SUBSTITUTE THAI FISH SAUCE)
1 TSP. FRESHLY GROUND BLACK PEPPER
SALT
7 TBSP. BUTTER, IN SMALL CUBES

TOPPING
HANDFUL OF SPINACH
1 CLOVE GARLIC, CRUSHED
3 ½ TBSP. BUTTER
SALT AND FRESHLY GROUND BLACK PEPPER
2 TBSP. OLIVE OIL
4 TO 6 PIECES OF POACHED FISH (OPTIONAL)

HARIRA

This recipe is enough for a bit more than 4 to 6 bowls, so either make it for a dinner party or freeze the extra.

Grate the onion and the tomato on a coarse grater. Chop the cilantro, parsley, and celery leaves very finely. In a large soup pan, heat the olive oil with the onion, tomato, smen, black peppercorns, ginger, ras el hanout, cinnamon stick, turmeric, pepper, and salt. Sauté until the spices release their fragrance. Then add the finely chopped herbs, lentils, fava beans, and chickpeas. Add 6 cups of water, bring to a boil, then simmer gently for 45 minutes. Once the lentils and chickpeas are fully cooked, stir the tomato paste and rice into the soup. When the rice is cooked, you can make the tadouira (traditional blend of flour and water) to bind the soup; it will make the soup nice and velvety. To do this, in a bowl, stir the flour with 5 tablespoons of water to make a smooth paste and add this mixture in a thin stream to the soup while continuing to stir. Return the soup to a boil. Once the foam is no longer white, everything is cooked.

Pour the soup into bowls and garnish with some parsley, if desired. Put some vinegar and lemon wedges on the table so everyone can season their own soup.

1 LARGE ONION
4 RIPE TOMATOES
½ BUNCH OF CILANTRO (MORE THAN THE PARSLEY)
½ BUNCH OF FLAT-LEAF PARSLEY
1 LARGE HANDFUL OF CELERY LEAVES
7 TBSP. OLIVE OIL
1 TBSP. SMEN (MOROCCAN FERMENTED BUTTER) OR REGULAR BUTTER
1 TBSP. BLACK PEPPERCORNS
1 ½ TSP. GROUND GINGER
1 ½ TSP. RAS EL HANOUT (AVAILABLE ONLINE)

1 CINNAMON STICK
1 ½ TSP. GROUND TURMERIC
1 TSP. FRESHLY GROUND BLACK PEPPER
1 TSP. SALT
⅓ CUP BROWN LENTILS
½ CUP FRESH SHELLED FAVA BEANS
¾ CUP CANNED CHICKPEAS
¼ CUP TOMATO PASTE
¼ CUP RICE, RINSED
2 TBSP. FLOUR

TOPPING
½ BUNCH FLAT-LEAF PARSLEY, FINELY CHOPPED (OPTIONAL)
VINEGAR
LEMON WEDGES

NOODLES IN BEEF BROTH

Brown the beef shank over medium-high heat all around in a heavy pan with the sunflower oil. Add the onions and garlic and sauté until translucent. Add the tomato paste, tomatoes, ginger, star anise, cinnamon sticks, Szechuan pepper, doubanjiang, soy sauce, Shaoxing rice wine, and 2 ½ quarts of water. The ingredients should be only just submerged. Simmer on very low heat for at least 5 hours. Allow the soup to reduce by almost half. The meat will now fall off the bone. Remove the bones, star anise, and cinnamon sticks and season the soup with the palm sugar and rice vinegar.

To make the topping, in a second pan, cook the noodles until al dente according to package instructions. Cut the bok choy into ¾-inch pieces and cook for 3 minutes in the hot meat stock.

Divide the noodles among large bowls. Pour over the soup and garnish with the green onions and red chili. Add the shank to the soup of the person who might enjoy sucking out the marrow.

1 ⅓ POUNDS BEEF SHANK
2 TBSP. SUNFLOWER OIL,
  PLUS MORE AS NEEDED
2 ONIONS, GRATED
5 CLOVES GARLIC, FINELY CHOPPED
2 TBSP. TOMATO PASTE
4 TOMATOES, DICED (⅜- IN CUBES)
2-IN. PIECE FRESH GINGER,
  PEELED AND GRATED
5 STAR ANISE

2 CINNAMON STICKS
2 TSP. SZECHUAN PEPPER
2 TBSP. DOUBANJIANG (CHINESE
  BLACK BEAN CHILI PASTE)
½ CUP SOY SAUCE
½ CUP SHAOXING RICE WINE
  (OR SUBSTITUTE SHERRY)
1 TBSP. PALM SUGAR
  (OR SUBSTITUTE BROWN SUGAR)
2 TBSP. RICE VINEGAR

TOPPING
11 OUNCES WHEAT RAMEN NOODLES
1 BOK CHOY
3 GREEN ONIONS, FINELY CHOPPED
1 FRESH RED CHILI, FINELY CHOPPED

ZUPPA DI BACCALÀ

Soak the salted cod in cold water for 24 hours. Change the water every now and then so that the salt is drawn from the fish. Cut the desalted fish into 1 ¼-inch cubes.

Heat the olive oil in a pan over low heat. Reserve a few slices of celery for the garnish and add the rest with the garlic. Sauté for about 5 minutes, until the garlic browns slightly but does not burn. Add the dried red pepper to the pan, followed by the roasted pepper and tomatoes. Cover with a heavy lid and stew for 15 minutes, then add the cubed fish and fish stock. Add potatoes to the pan and simmer for another 30 minutes. Season the soup with salt, pepper, and lemon juice.

Pour the soup into bowls and garnish with the reserved celery, parsley, lemon zest, olives, and a generous splash of olive oil.

7 OUNCES SALT COD
7 TBSP. OLIVE OIL
2 CELERY RIBS, THINLY SLICED
6 CLOVES GARLIC, FINELY CHOPPED
1 TSP. DRIED RED PEPPER FLAKES
1 JARRED ROASTED RED
   PEPPER, DICED
1 ⅔ CUPS CANNED PEELED
   TOMATOES
2 ½ CUPS FISH STOCK
   (CHICKEN IS ALSO ACCEPTABLE)
1 CUP PEELED AND DICED POTATOES
SALT AND FRESHLY GROUND
   BLACK PEPPER
JUICE OF 1 LEMON

TOPPING
½ BUNCH OF FLAT-LEAF PARSLEY,
   FINELY CHOPPED
GRATED ZEST OF 1 ORGANIC LEMON
FEW BLACK OLIVES, HALVED
   AND PITTED
EXTRA-VIRGIN OLIVE OIL

RED CABBAGE SOUP WITH RICOTTA DUMPLINGS

Put the stock, pork shank, thyme, black peppercorns, bay leaf, red cabbage, onion, and celery in a large saucepan and simmer gently for 2 hours. Pour the contents of the pan through a strainer. Discard the solids.

Meanwhile, make the pickled red cabbage for the topping. Cut the red cabbage into thin strips and combine in a bowl with the apple cider vinegar, sugar, salt, and pepper. Make sure the red cabbage is submerged and let rest for 20 to 40 minutes, until softened.

Make the ricotta dumplings by mixing the ricotta, Parmesan cheese, egg yolks, white bread, ⅓ cup of the flour, pepper, salt, and nutmeg until cohesive. Put the remaining 1 ⅓ cups of flour in a deep dish. Using 2 spoons, form 12 to 15 balls of the ricotta mixture and roll them through the flour until completely coated. Place them in the refrigerator until the stock is ready.

Reheat the stock. In a separate large saucepan, bring 2 quarts of water to a gentle boil. Add the ricotta dumplings and cook for 3 to 5 minutes, until they float, and then gently scoop them out of the water with a slotted spoon. Place them in deep plates, pour the hot stock around them, and garnish with olive oil, parsley, pickled red cabbage, and the Parmesan cheese, if desired.

8 ½ CUPS VEGETABLE
   OR CHICKEN STOCK
1 PORK SHANK
3 SPRIGS OF THYME
10 BLACK PEPPERCORNS
1 BAY LEAF
9 OUNCES RED CABBAGE,
   COARSELY CHOPPED
1 ONION, HALVED
1 CELERY RIB, COARSELY CHOPPED

TOPPING
2 ¼ OUNCES RED CABBAGE
2 TBSP. APPLE CIDER VINEGAR
1 TBSP. SUGAR
SALT AND FRESHLY GROUND
   BLACK PEPPER

RICOTTA DUMPLINGS
11 OUNCES RICOTTA
¾ CUP FRESHLY GRATED
   PARMESAN CHEESE, PLUS MORE
   FOR GARNISH (OPTIONAL)
2 EGG YOLKS
1 SLICE OF STALE WHITE BREAD,
   SOAKED IN MILK, DRAINED,
   AND CRUMBLED
1 ⅔ CUPS FLOUR
PINCH OF NUTMEG
4 TO 6 TBSP. OLIVE OIL
PARSLEY LEAVES, FOR GARNISH

COLD BEET SOUP

WITH PURPLE BASIL AND BLACKBERRIES

Mix the raspberry vinegar, reduced beet juice, balsamic vinegar, orange juice, sherry vinegar, maple syrup, mustard, and a pinch of salt until smooth in a saucepan. Place the soup in the refrigerator until you are ready to serve.

To make the topping, cook the beets in a pan of salted water until you can easily push through them with a skewer. This will take at least 20 minutes. Scoop the beets out of the water, drain, and let them cool slightly. Then you can easily peel off the outer skin.

In a bowl, mash the blackberries, cherries, and black currants with a fork. Transfer to a saucepan, add the lemon juice and zest, oyster sauce, celery, red chili, and Thai basil leaves and simmer gently for 1 minute. It is also an option not to cook it but let it marinate for 30 minutes at most.

Divide the fruit among four deep plates, place three small, peeled beets in each plate, and spoon a tablespoon of crème fraîche on top. Pour the soup around it. Serve with the salmon, if desired.

2 TBSP. RASPBERRY VINEGAR
4 ¼ CUPS BEET JUICE, BOILED DOWN
 TO ABOUT 1 CUP
1 ½ TBSP. BALSAMIC VINEGAR
JUICE OF 1 ORANGE
1 ½ TBSP. SHERRY VINEGAR
9 TBSP. MAPLE SYRUP
1 ½ TBSP. COARSE MUSTARD
SALT

TOPPING
12 SMALL RED BEETS
½ CUP BLACKBERRIES
½ CUP PITTED CHERRIES
½ CUP BLACK CURRANTS
GRATED ZEST AND JUICE OF ½
 ORGANIC LEMON
2 TBSP. OYSTER SAUCE
1 CELERY RIB, DICED INTO
 ⅛-IN. CUBES

½ FRESH RED CHILI, SEEDED AND
 FINELY CHOPPED
4 SPRIGS OF PURPLE THAI BASIL,
 LEAVES ONLY
¼ CUP CRÈME FRAÎCHE
COLD-SMOKED SALMON, THINLY SLICED
 (OPTIONAL)

ROASTED VITELOTTE POTATO SOUP WITH GOAT CHEESE

Preheat the oven to 400°F.

Coarsely chop the potatoes and red onion. Pull the cloves off the garlic bulb. Place everything on a baking sheet lined with parchment paper. Pour half of the olive oil on top. Add the sprigs of rosemary and sprinkle with salt and pepper. Mix well. Cover the baking sheet completely with aluminum foil to keep the steam from escaping. Bake in the oven for 50 minutes, until the potatoes are tender.

When the potatoes are almost cooked, put a pan with the vegetable stock on low heat.

Remove the garlic and rosemary. Scrape the potatoes and red onion with any juices from the baking sheet into a blender, or transfer to a saucepan and use an immersion blender. While blending until smooth, pour in the stock in three additions. When the soup is completely smooth, add the rest of the olive oil and blend the soup one last time.

In a pan with the olive oil, roast the carrots, leek, and rosemary for the topping until tender. Pour the hot soup into bowls and crumble the goat cheese on top. Garnish with the carrot, leek, and rosemary. Finish with a few drops of olive oil and more black pepper to taste.

1 ½ POUNDS VITELOTTE POTATOES OR OTHER BLUE-PURPLE POTATOES
7 OUNCES RED ONION
1 BULB GARLIC, UNPEELED
9 TBSP. OLIVE OIL
5 SPRIGS OF ROSEMARY
COARSE SEA SALT AND FRESHLY GROUND BLACK PEPPER
4 ¼ CUPS VEGETABLE STOCK

TOPPING
2 TBSP. OLIVE OIL, PLUS MORE AS NEEDED
2 CARROTS, PEELED AND COARSELY CHOPPED
½ LEEK, SLICED
4 SPRIGS OF ROSEMARY
3 TO 4 OUNCES GOAT CHEESE (CHÈVRE)
FRESHLY GROUND BLACK PEPPER

BORSCHT

In a heavy pan, sauté the soup bones in the sunflower oil. Add the bay leaf and thyme, deglaze with 8 cups of water, and bring to a boil. Season with quite a bit of pepper. Cook for 3 hours on low heat, until the meat falls off the bone. Scoop the bones from the pan and strain the stock. You can discard the leftover flavorings. Let the bones cool and pluck the meat.

Sauté the shallots over medium-high heat in a large pan with the butter. Add the potatoes, beets, and kohlrabi to the shallots in the pan and pour in the stock. Bring to a boil and simmer for 20 minutes. Add the plucked meat, carrots, celery, and leeks along with the cabbage and garlic to the soup. Cook for another 10 minutes and season the soup with the red wine vinegar, salt, and pepper.

Pour the soup into bowls and finish with a tablespoon of crème fraîche, a few drops of olive oil, and some dill.

2 ¼ POUNDS BEEF SOUP BONES
3 TBSP. SUNFLOWER OIL
1 BAY LEAF
5 SPRIGS OF THYME
2 SHALLOTS, FINELY CHOPPED
3 ½ TBSP. BUTTER
1 ⅓ CUPS POTATOES, PEELED AND DICED (⅜-IN. CUBES)
2 ¼ CUPS RAW BEETS, PEELED AND DICED (⅜-IN. CUBES)

1 CUP KOHLRABI, PEELED AND DICED (⅜-IN. CUBES)
1 CUP CARROTS, PEELED AND DICED (⅜-IN. CUBES)
1 CELERY RIB, DICED (⅜-IN. CUBES)
1 CUP LEEKS, THINLY SLICED
3 CUPS SHREDDED GREEN CABBAGE
2 CLOVES GARLIC, FINELY CHOPPED
2 TBSP. RED WINE VINEGAR
SALT AND FRESHLY GROUND BLACK PEPPER

TOPPING
4 TO 6 TBSP. CRÈME FRAÎCHE
2 TBSP. OLIVE OIL
½ BUNCH OF DILL, FINELY CHOPPED

PURPLE SWEET POTATO SOUP

Heat the olive oil in a large pan over medium-high heat and sauté the onion, celery, garlic, ras el hanout, and ginger for a few minutes. Add the sweet potatoes and sauté for a few more minutes. Deglaze with the vegetable stock and coconut milk. Bring to a boil and simmer for 30 minutes. When the sweet potatoes are fully cooked, transfer the soup to a blender or use an immersion blender and process until the soup is smooth.

For the topping, blister the red chilis under the broiler or over the open flame of the stove until black and soft. Peel off the skin and remove the seeds. Toast the caraway seeds in 2 tablespoons of the olive oil until fragrant. Add the garlic and tomato paste and sauté for a moment. Combine the contents of the pan along with the chilis in a blender and add the rose water, red wine vinegar, and 4 tablespoons of the olive oil. Blend into a smooth harissa oil and season with salt. Pour into a small bowl. Clean the blender and add the cilantro, parsley, and remaining 7 tablespoons of olive oil. Blend into a smooth green herb oil.

Serve the soup hot with a generous tablespoon of both oils in each bowl and some finely chopped preserved lemon zest and toasted almonds.

3 TBSP. OLIVE OIL
1 RED ONION, GRATED
2 CELERY RIBS, THINLY SLICED
4 CLOVES GARLIC, FINELY CHOPPED
1 TBSP. RAS EL HANOUT
1 ¼-IN. FRESH GINGER, PEELED AND FINELY CHOPPED
1 ⅔ POUNDS PURPLE SWEET POTATOES, PEELED AND DICED
5 CUPS VEGETABLE STOCK
¾ CUPS COCONUT MILK

TOPPING
2 FRESH RED CHILIS
2 TSP. CARAWAY SEEDS
13 TBSP. OLIVE OIL
2 CLOVES GARLIC, FINELY CHOPPED
2 TSP. TOMATO PASTE
1 TBSP. ROSE WATER
1 ½ TBSP. RED WINE VINEGAR
SALT
HANDFUL OF CILANTRO, FINELY CHOPPED

SMALL HANDFUL OF FLAT-LEAF PARSLEY, FINELY CHOPPED
1 PRESERVED LEMON, ZEST FINELY CHOPPED
HANDFUL OF TOASTED ALMONDS, FINELY CHOPPED

GREEN GAZPACHO WITH BURRATA

Coarsely chop the tomatoes, cucumber, bell peppers, onion, and avocados. Combine in a blender with the spinach, ginger, chilis, garlic, mint, basil, cilantro, cumin seeds, rice vinegar, and olive oil. Process until you have a smooth soup. Pour the gazpacho through a fine strainer. If necessary, push the last remaining soup through the strainer with the rounded side of a spoon and season with salt. Let the soup chill thoroughly in the refrigerator for at least 1 hour.

Pour the gazpacho into bowls and finish with some burrata, avocado, cucumber strips, and a mix of fresh green herbs.

10 YELLOW TOMATOES
1 CUCUMBER, PEELED
2 GREEN BELL PEPPERS, SEEDED
1 ONION
2 AVOCADOS, PEELED AND PITTED
1 HANDFUL OF RAW SPINACH
   (FOR COLOR)
2 TBSP. FRESH GINGER, PEELED
   AND FINELY CHOPPED
1 ½ GREEN CHILIS, SEEDED
3 CLOVES GARLIC, FINELY CHOPPED
4 SPRIGS OF MINT, LEAVES ONLY
1 BUNCH OF BASIL, LEAVES ONLY
1 BUNCH OF CILANTRO, LEAVES ONLY
2 TBSP. CUMIN SEEDS, TOASTED
¾ CUP RICE VINEGAR
1 ⅔ CUP OLIVE OIL
SALT

TOPPING
1 TO 2 BALLS OF BURRATA, TORN
1 AVOCADO, PEELED, PITTED,
   AND THINLY SLICED
¼ CUCUMBER, IN LONG THIN STRIPS
1 BUNCH OF FRESH GREEN HERBS,
   PREFERABLY A MIX, FINELY CHOPPED

DUTCH SPLIT PEA SOUP

Dutch Split Pea Soup is never cooked in small portions. Therefore, in a large saucepan, combine the pork shank and split peas with 4 quarts of water and bring to a boil, skimming off any impurities that bubble to the surface with a skimmer if necessary. When no more foam bubbles up, add the pork belly.

Simmer gently for 1 ½ to 2 hours, until the split peas break up. Stir frequently so that the split peas do not crumble to the bottom.

Add the celeriac, parsnip, leeks, and celery leaves to the soup. Grate the potato on a fine grater and add with the smoked sausage. Boil the pea soup for 20 minutes and season with salt and pepper. Remove the pork shank, pork belly, and smoked sausage from the soup. Slice the smoked sausage. Chop the meat from the pork shank and return to the soup with the smoked sausage. Keep the pork belly behind.

Pea soup and snert (Dutch Split Pea Soup) are the same in terms of ingredients, but snert is only proper snert if it has been allowed to rest overnight before consumption. That way, all the flavors get properly infused, and the texture is optimal.

Slice the pork belly. It can be trimmed and eaten cold with the soup, served on a slice of rye bread with a thick layer of butter. Ladle the soup into bowls and garnish with the parsley and some pepper.

1 POUND BONE-IN PORK SHANK
2 CUPS SPLIT PEAS
5 ¼ OUNCES PORK BELLY
½ CELERIAC, PEELED AND FINELY
  CHOPPED
1 PARSNIP, PEELED AND FINELY
  CHOPPED
5 CUPS FINELY CHOPPED LEEKS, FINELY
  CHOPPED
1 LARGE HANDFUL OF CELERY LEAVES,
  FINELY CHOPPED
2 POTATOES, PEELED
8 OUNCES COARSE-TEXTURED SMOKED
  SAUSAGE
SALT AND FRESHLY GROUND BLACK
  PEPPER

TOPPING
4 TO 6 SLICES OF RYE BREAD
  WITH BUTTER (OR MORE)
1 BUNCH OF FLAT-LEAF PARSLEY,
  FINELY CHOPPED
FRESHLY GROUND BLACK PEPPER

GREEN ASPARAGUS AND PEA SOUP

WITH A SALAD OF HARICOTS VERTS AND ALMONDS

In a large saucepan, combine the stock, asparagus, milk, and cream and bring to a boil. Add the peas and spinach and return to a boil. Transfer the soup to a blender and process until smooth, or use an immersion blender. Strain the soup through a fine strainer. If necessary, push the last remaining soup through the sieve with the rounded side of a spoon. Using an immersion blender, blend the butter into the soup. Season the soup with salt, sugar, and lemon juice. Keep warm over low heat.

For the salad topping, cut off the tips and tails of the green beans. Cook the green beans until crisp-tender in a pan with plenty of salted water. After 4 minutes of cooking, transfer them into a bowl of ice water so they cool quickly and retain their beautiful color.

In a large skillet, melt the butter. Let it bubble for a moment, then add the green beans. Simmer them in the butter for 5 minutes, then add the almonds. Let the almonds brown nicely in the bubbling butter for 3 to 4 minutes. Then add the lemon juice and thyme leaves. Season with salt.

Place the salad in a heap in a bowl or deep plate and pour the hot soup around it. Drizzle with the olive oil.

4 ¼ CUPS VEGETABLE OR
  CHICKEN STOCK
2 ¼ POUNDS GREEN ASPARAGUS,
  COARSELY CHOPPED AND
  WOODY ENDS DISCARDED
1 CUP WHOLE MILK
1 CUP LIGHT CREAM
1 POUND SHELLED PEAS
  (FRESH OR FROZEN)
3 ½ OUNCES SPINACH
7 TBSP. BUTTER
SALT
PINCH OF SUGAR
JUICE OF 1 LEMON

TOPPING
1 POUND GREEN BEANS
1 ½ TBSP. BUTTER
⅔ CUP COARSELY CHOPPED
  ALMONDS
JUICE OF 1 LEMON
3 SPRIGS OF THYME, JUST THE LEAVES
SALT
2 TBSP. OLIVE OIL

ZUCCHINI AND BREAD SOUP

In a large pan with the olive oil, sauté the garlic until it browns. Be careful not to burn the slices. Once the garlic is browned, add the onions, zucchini, thyme, and celery and turn the heat down to low. Cover the pan and simmer gently for 30 minutes. If you are afraid of the ingredients sticking to the pan, add a dash of vegetable stock. After the 30 minutes have passed, add the rest of the vegetable stock and bring to a boil. Reduce the stock by a quarter to make a thick, lumpy soup. Mix the bread into the soup and season with plenty of pepper, some salt, and the lemon zest. You can leave the soup coarse, or you can puree some or all of it. Don't be stingy with the toppings!

Make a quick basil oil in a mortar by grinding the basil leaves with the olive oil. Divide the soup among deep plates containing the matchsticks of zucchini and squeeze a little lemon juice over each plate. Sprinkle with the Parmesan cheese, then sprinkle with the lemon zest and drizzle with some more olive oil and the basil oil.

7 TBSP. OLIVE OIL
5 CLOVES GARLIC, THINLY SLICED
2 ONIONS, GRATED
2 ½ ZUCCHINI, COARSELY DICED
2 SPRIGS OF THYME
2 CELERY RIBS, DICED (⅓-IN. CUBES)
5 CUPS VEGETABLE STOCK
3 ½ OUNCES HEARTY (SOURDOUGH) STALE BREAD WITHOUT CRUSTS, CUT INTO ¾-IN. CUBES
SALT AND FRESHLY GROUND BLACK PEPPER
GRATED ZEST OF 1 ORGANIC LEMON

TOPPING
½ BUNCH OF BASIL, JUST THE LEAVES
4 TBSP. OLIVE OIL, PLUS MORE TO DRIZZLE
GRATED ZEST AND JUICE OF 1 ORGANIC LEMON
½ ZUCCHINI, CUT IN MATCHSTICKS
½ CUP GRATED PARMESAN CHEESE

GREEN CURRY SOUP ^{WITH BROCCOLI}

Let's start by making the curry paste. In a dry skillet over medium-high heat, toast the coriander seeds, cumin seeds, and white peppercorns until fragrant. Let cool and grind them in a mortar or spice grinder to a fine powder. Remove from the mortar or grinder and grind the remaining ingredients for the curry paste in a large mortar or food processor. Add all the ground ingredients together.

Sauté the curry paste in a large pan over medium-high heat until the oil separates from it. Add the palm sugar, coconut milk, and coconut cream. Allow to simmer just below boiling point for 20 minutes. If you have a kitchen thermometer, aim for 200°F. Add the spinach, allow it to wilt for a moment. Transfer the curry to a blender, or use an immersion blender, and process until smooth. Then pour through a fine-mesh strainer for even smoother results. If necessary, push the last remaining curry through the sieve with the rounded side of a spoon.

In a skillet, fry the broccoli, mushrooms, and eggplant for a few minutes until al dente and add them to the soup. Garnish with the Thai basil leaves.

CURRY PASTE
1 TBSP. CORIANDER SEEDS
1 ½ TSP. CUMIN SEEDS
½ TSP. WHITE PEPPERCORNS
⅔ CUP FINELY CHOPPED SHALLOTS
¼ CUP STEMMED, PEELED, AND
   MINCED GALANGAL
4 LEMONGRASS STALKS, INNER PART
   FINELY CHOPPED
4 CLOVES GARLIC, FINELY CHOPPED
4 MAKRUT LIME LEAVES, VEINS
   REMOVED AND FINELY CHOPPED
GRATED ZEST OF 1 MAKRUT LIME
8 TO 10 GREEN CHILIS (OR TO TASTE),
   HALF SEEDED
PINCH OF SALT

SOUP
3 ½ TBSP. PALM SUGAR
   (OR SUBSTITUTE BROWN SUGAR)
4 ¼ CUPS COCONUT MILK
2 CUPS COCONUT CREAM
8 OUNCES SPINACH
BROCCOLI CROWN, CUT INTO FLORETS
10 WHITE MUSHROOMS, SLICED
½ EGGPLANT, DICED (⅜-IN. CUBES)
   THAI BASIL LEAVES (OPTIONAL)

CALDO VERDE WITH CHORIZO

In a deep, heavy pan, sauté the onions and garlic in the olive oil until soft and translucent. Strip the chorizo of its skin and cut into coarse pieces. Sauté the chorizo with the smoked paprika for a few minutes. Coarsely chop the potatoes and add to the pan along with the chicken stock, bay leaves, and kale. Simmer for a good 15 minutes. The potato pieces should be cooked through and may fall apart. This will ensure some thickening of the soup. Season with salt and pepper to taste.

Serve the soup with a splash of good olive oil and some pieces of toasted bread.

2 ONIONS, GRATED
4 CLOVES GARLIC, FINELY CHOPPED
4 TBSP. OLIVE OIL
5 ¼ OUNCES SPANISH CURED
  CHORIZO
½ TSP. SMOKED PAPRIKA
6 BAKING POTATOES, PEELED
6 ⅓ CUPS CHICKEN STOCK
2 BAY LEAVES
9 ½ CUPS STEMMED AND FINELY
  CHOPPED KALE
SALT AND FRESHLY GROUND
  BLACK PEPPER

TOPPING
4 TO 6 TBSP. EXTRA-VIRGIN OLIVE OIL
4 TO 6 SLICES OF HEARTY
  (SOURDOUGH) BREAD,
  LIGHTLY TOASTED

WATERCRESS SOUP

Heat the olive oil in a heavy pan and sauté the onion and celery in it for a few minutes. Add the stock and potatoes, both diced and whole. Bring to a boil and simmer for 25 minutes so that the potatoes are fully cooked. Remove the whole potato from the pan and set aside. Stir the watercress and crème fraîche into the soup. Simmer for about 3 minutes, then process in a blender, or with an immersion blender, until smooth. Season with nutmeg, salt, and pepper.

To make the topping, in a bowl, mix the grated horseradish with the crème fraîche. Cut the reserved cooked potato into small cubes.

Pour the hot soup into bowls and garnish with some cubed potatoes, horseradish crème fraîche, shrimp, and watercress. Sprinkle the lemon zest over it. Finish with a grind of pepper.

¼ CUP OLIVE OIL
1 ONION, GRATED
1 CELERY RIB, DICED
2 ½ CUPS FISH, SHELLFISH, OR CHICKEN STOCK
2 ¼ CUPS PEELED AND DICED POTATOES, PLUS 1 WHOLE PEELED POTATO
7 OUNCES WATERCRESS
7 TBSP. CRÈME FRAÎCHE
PINCH OF NUTMEG
SALT AND FRESHLY GROUND BLACK PEPPER

TOPPING
2 TSP. GRATED FRESH HORSERADISH
6 TBSP. CRÈME FRAÎCHE
5 ¼ OUNCES PEELED, COOKED SMALL SHRIMP
HANDFUL OF WATERCRESS OR GARDEN CRESS
GRATED ZEST OF ½ TO 1 ORGANIC LEMON
FRESHLY GROUND BLACK PEPPER

PARSLEY AND WILD GARLIC SOUP ^{WITH SNAILS}

This recipe makes enough for two hungry eaters.

Heat the butter in a large pan over medium-high heat and sauté the onions and garlic for a few minutes. Add the peppercorns, bay leaf, and thyme and sauté for a moment. Deglaze with the vermouth and reduce the volume to 10 percent. Pour the cream, milk, and chicken stock into the pan, bring to a boil, and simmer over low heat for 1 hour. Strain the stock through a clean cheesecloth, creating a creamy liquid with no solids. Season with salt to taste.

To make the topping, in a blender, combine the wild garlic, parsley, and sunflower oil and process for 10 minutes so that the consistency is as smooth as possible. Strain over a bowl if you want a clear oil.

Heat a dash of sunflower oil in a grill pan over medium-high heat and cook the zucchini slices for a few minutes until tender and marked by the grill. Heat a layer of sunflower oil in a skillet over medium-high heat and deep-fry the garlic slices until light brown and crispy. Drain on paper towels.

Warm the cooked snails in the soup. Pour into bowls and garnish with the parsley and wild garlic oil, zucchini, and fried garlic.

3 ½ TBSP. BUTTER
3 WHITE ONIONS, CHOPPED
4 CLOVES GARLIC, FINELY CHOPPED
10 BLACK PEPPERCORNS
1 BAY LEAF
1 SPRIG OF THYME
7 TBSP. NOILLY PRAT OR OTHER
   DRY VERMOUTH
2 CUPS LIGHT CREAM
2 CUPS WHOLE MILK
1 CUP CHICKEN STOCK
SALT

TOPPING
1 BUNCH OF WILD GARLIC
   (OR SUBSTITUTE WILD LEEKS)
1 BUNCH OF CURLY PARSLEY
1 CUP SUNFLOWER OIL,
   PLUS MORE AS NEEDED
1 BABY ZUCCHINI, IN LONG SLICES
1 CLOVE GARLIC, THINLY SLICED
12 COOKED SNAILS, 6 PER PERSON

ONION SOUP

Cut the onions into thin slices. Fry them with the butter in a large pan over low heat for about 20 minutes until they begin to brown. Cut the bacon into cubes. Tie the herbs together with kitchen twine and add to the pan. The pan may now be placed on high heat. Fry the bacon for a few minutes. Pour in the port and balsamic vinegar. Stir well to loosen any browned bits from the bottom of the pan. Add the chicken stock. Season to taste with salt and pepper. Simmer everything for about 1 hour. When the soup begins to foam, skim it off with a slotted spoon. After an hour, scoop the bundle of herbs out of the pan.

Preheat the broiler.

Pour the soup into ovenproof bowls. Toast the slices of baguette in a pan with the olive oil until crispy. Divide the baguette croutons among the bowls of soup, topping with the Gruyère. Place the bowls under the broiler until the cheese melts and browns. If you do not have ovenproof bowls, you can place the croutons on a baking sheet lined with parchment paper and spread the cheese over the croutons. Broil until golden brown and then place them on top of the hot soup.

6 LARGE ONIONS
7 TBSP. BUTTER
5 ¼ OUNCES SMOKED BACON
2 SPRIGS OF FLAT-LEAF PARSLEY
3 SPRIGS OF THYME
2 BAY LEAVES
3 TBSP. PORT
3 TBSP. HIGH-QUALITY
   BALSAMIC VINEGAR
6 ⅓ CUPS CHICKEN STOCK
SALT AND FRESHLY GROUND
   BLACK PEPPER

TOPPING
8 SLICES OF BAGUETTE
4 TBSP. OLIVE OIL
1 ½ CUPS SHREDDED GRUYÈRE

CHICKEN SOUP

Cut the legs from the chicken, as well as the wings and breasts. Chop the carcass into three pieces. Put a large pan with 7 cups of water on the stove and add the chicken legs, wings, and carcass. Put the breasts in the refrigerator. Cut 1 of the leeks, the onion, and carrot in halves lengthwise and add to the pan along with the whole tomato. Also add the celery, the bay leaves, peppercorns, mace, herbes de Provence, oregano, parsley, and celery leaves and bring to a boil. Turn down the heat and let the stock simmer for 4 hours with the lid on the pan. Skim off the impurities that bubble up regularly with a slotted spoon.

Remove the pan from the heat and strain the stock. Pick the meat from the chicken legs and wings in fine pieces and add these to the stock. The rest of the flavorings, including the vegetables, may be discarded. Place the stock in the refrigerator overnight. The following day, carefully remove the layer of solidified fat with some paper towels.

Pour the chicken stock into a large saucepan. Cut the reserved breasts into small, thin strips. Cut the white of the second leek into thin rings. Break the stalks off the mushrooms. Clean the caps with paper towels. Cut the mushrooms into quarters. Add the chicken breast, leeks, and mushroom caps and stems to the chicken stock and warm slowly. After the stock has boiled gently for 5 minutes, the chicken pieces should be cooked through. Season the chicken soup with salt and garnish with the celery leaves.

1 WHOLE CHICKEN (3.5 POUNDS)
2 LEEKS
1 LARGE WHITE ONION
½ LARGE CARROT
1 TOMATO
3 CELERY RIBS, COARSELY CHOPPED
3 BAY LEAVES
5 BLACK PEPPERCORNS
1 TSP. MACE

1 TBSP. HERBES DE PROVENCE
1 TBSP. DRIED OREGANO
3 SPRIGS OF FLAT-LEAF PARSLEY
3 SPRIGS OF CELERY LEAVES
4 ½ OUNCES SMALL WHITE
  MUSHROOMS
SALT AND FRESHLY GROUND
  BLACK PEPPER

TOPPING
1 SMALL HANDFUL OF CELERY LEAVES,
  FINELY CHOPPED

PEANUT SOUP

Rub the chicken thighs generously with salt and let brine in the refrigerator for at least 2 hours.

In a large saucepan, bring the vegetable stock to a boil. Cut the potato into ⅜-inch cubes. Trim the yardlong beans and cut into ¾-inch pieces. Cook the potato and yardlong beans in the stock until crisp-tender. Scoop them out of the pan with a slotted spoon and set aside.

In a large pan, sauté the chicken thighs in the sunflower oil. Add the onion, garlic, ginger, lime leaves, lemongrass, coriander seeds, and sambal oelek and fry for a while. Add the flour and continue to fry for a moment. Deglaze the pan with the stock. Add the peanut butter, kecap manis, and coconut milk. Let simmer slowly for at least 40 minutes. Stir occasionally. You can serve the chicken whole or scoop it out and pluck the meat off the bone. Season the soup with salt and pepper.

Divide the chicken, potato, beans, and, if desired, the bean sprouts among the bowls. Pour the hot peanut soup over it. Garnish with the lime juice, celery leaves, kecap manis, and fried onions, if desired.

4 BONE-IN CHICKEN THIGHS
4 ¼ CUPS VEGETABLE STOCK
3 ¼ OUNCES POTATO, PEELED
3 ¼ OUNCES YARDLONG BEANS
   (OR SUBSTITUTE GREEN BEANS)
3 TBSP. SUNFLOWER OIL
1 ONION, GRATED
2 CLOVES GARLIC, FINELY CHOPPED
2 TSP. PEELED AND GRATED
   FRESH GINGER
2 MAKRUT LIME LEAVES, VEINS
   REMOVED AND VERY THINLY SLICED
2 LEMONGRASS STALKS, INNER
   PART FINELY CHOPPED

1 TSP. CORIANDER SEEDS
1 TBSP. SAMBAL OELEK
   (OR SUBSTITUTE A DIFFERENT
   CHILI PASTE)
2 TBSP. FLOUR
¼ CUP PEANUT BUTTER
3 TBSP. KECAP MANIS (OR
   SUBSTITUTE SWEET SOY SAUCE)
1 ¼ CUPS COCONUT MILK
SALT AND FRESHLY GROUND
   BLACK PEPPER
2 CUPS MUNG BEAN SPROUTS
   (OPTIONAL)

TOPPING
JUICE OF 1 LIME
1 SMALL HANDFUL OF CELERY LEAVES,
   FINELY CHOPPED
1 TBSP. KECAP MANIS
   (OR SUBSTITUTE SWEET SOY SAUCE)
4 TO 6 TBSP. FRIED ONIONS
   (OPTIONAL)

SURINAMESE BROWN BEAN SOUP

Boil the salt pork in 7 cups of water to desalt it a bit.

Cook just until tender, about 30 minutes. Taste to see if enough salt has boiled out (it should be as salty as cured meat, but not overly salty), otherwise let it cook a little longer. Remove any excess fat and cut the salt pork into small pieces.

In a large pan with sunflower oil, sauté the onion and tomatoes. Add the tomato paste and sauté for a moment. Add the celery leaves to the pan along with the pinto beans. Allow to heat gently. Season the chicken thighs with salt and pepper and fry in a pan with some sunflower oil until nicely browned. Put the chicken thighs into the pan with the pinto beans, along with the salt pork. Pick the meat off the smoked cooked chicken leg and add to the pan. Pour in the chicken stock and simmer for 30 minutes with the whole chili added. Please note! The chili should not be broken, it is only about the aroma, not the spiciness. The soup should be a little thick, not watery.

Pour the soup into bowls, divide the chicken thighs (bone-in or boneless) on top and finish with a tablespoon of piccalilli or sambal and the celery leaves.

11 OUNCES SALT PORK
2 TBSP. SUNFLOWER OIL,
   PLUS MORE AS NEEDED
1 LARGE ONION, GRATED
3 TOMATOES, DICED (⅜-IN. CUBES)
⅓ CUP TOMATO PASTE
1 LARGE HANDFUL OF CELERY LEAVES,
   FINELY CHOPPED
3 ½ (15-OUNCE) CANS PINTO

BEANS WITH LIQUID
2 BONE-IN CHICKEN THIGHS
SALT AND FRESHLY GROUND
   BLACK PEPPER
1 SMOKED COOKED CHICKEN LEG
2 CUPS CHICKEN STOCK
1 MADAME JEANETTE CHILI
   (LEMON HABANERO)

TOPPING
4 TO 6 TBSP. PICCALILLI
   (MUSTARD PICKLE RELISH) OR
   SAMBAL OELEK, OR TO TASTE
LEAVES OF 1 CELERY HEAD

MUSHROOM CREAM SOUP

In a large saucepan, heat the stock with the dried porcini. In a second (tall) pan, sauté the onions and garlic in the butter and simmer for 10 minutes until completely soft. Add the chestnut mushrooms and turn the heat to high. Sauté until the moisture of the mushrooms has evaporated as much as possible. Set aside a few mushrooms for garnish. Scoop the remaining porcini out of the stock with a slotted spoon and sauté these, too, in the same pan with the mushrooms. Add the flour and cook with the mushrooms for a few minutes, stirring. Deglaze the pan with the stock and bring to a boil. Add the bay leaf. Simmer for a good 15 minutes. Fish the bay leaf from the soup and add the crème fraîche or cream. Transfer the soup to a blender, or use an immersion blender, and process until smooth. Season with salt, pepper, and the soy sauce. You can also strain the soup if you really want it to be completely smooth.

For the topping, cut the white bread into ⅜-inch cubes. Fry in a skillet with the olive oil until crispy. When the croutons are just about crispy, sprinkle the Parmesan cheese over them and shake the pan briefly.

Serve the soup with the Parmesan croutons, reserved mushrooms, and parsley.

5 CUPS CHICKEN OR
  VEGETABLE STOCK
SMALL HANDFUL OF DRIED PORCINI
  (OR OTHER DRIED MUSHROOMS)
2 ONIONS, GRATED
1 CLOVE GARLIC, FINELY CHOPPED
7 TBSP. BUTTER
1 ½ POUNDS CHESTNUT
  MUSHROOMS, COARSELY CHOPPED

2 TBSP. FLOUR
1 BAY LEAF
3 TBSP. CRÈME FRAÎCHE
  OR LIGHT CREAM
1 TBSP. SOY SAUCE
SALT AND FRESHLY GROUND
  BLACK PEPPER

TOPPING
2 SLICES OF STALE WHITE BREAD
3 TBSP. OLIVE OIL
¼ CUP FRESHLY GRATED
  PARMESAN CHEESE
4 SPRIGS OF FLAT-LEAF PARSLEY,
  FINELY CHOPPED

BEEF AND VEGETABLE SOUP

Put the meat in a large saucepan with 4 cups cold water and bring to a boil. Drain as soon as the water begins to boil. This is how you remove the impurities from the meat. In a clean pot, add the beef stock and bring the meat back to a slow boil. Simmer gently for 2 to 3 hours (do not boil). Remove the meat from the bone, cut into pieces, and return the meat to the stock.

In a large skillet with olive oil, sauté the onion with the carrots, cauliflower, leek, parsley, and celery leaves. When the stock is ready, add the vegetables and herbs to the pan, along with the rest of the spices. If necessary, season some more with pepper.

9 OUNCES BEEF SHANK
8 ½ CUPS BEEF STOCK
2 TBSP. OLIVE OIL
1 ONION, GRATED
2 CARROTS, IN SMALL CUBES
¼ CAULIFLOWER, IN SMALL FLORETS
1 LEEK, THINLY SLICED RINGS
½ BUNCH OF FLAT-LEAF PARSLEY, FINELY CHOPPED

1 SMALL HANDFUL OF CELERY LEAVES, FINELY CHOPPED
2 TSP. MACE
2 TSP. CORIANDER SEEDS
1 TSP. GROUND NUTMEG
1 TSP. FRESHLY GROUND BLACK PEPPER, PLUS MORE AS NEEDED

BROWN WINDSOR

Dredge the beef shank in the flour. Shake off any excess flour. Sprinkle with salt. Heat the butter in a heavy skillet and sauté the floured beef shank for a few minutes. The meat should brown, but the butter should not burn. Add the onion and garlic and sauté for a moment. Add about 6 cups of water and the marmite. Simmer, covered, on very low heat for 1 ½ hours. Stir well from time to time.

Tie the rosemary, sage, and bay leaf together with a piece of butcher's twine and add to the soup. Add the parsnip, carrots, and pearl barley to the soup and simmer for another 30 minutes. Remove the shank and the bundle of herbs from the soup. Let the meat cool, cut it into cubes, and then return it to the soup. Season the soup with salt, pepper, and Worcestershire sauce to taste.

To make the topping, put the chili rings in a bowl. Heat the white wine vinegar and 3 tablespoons of water with the sugar and a pinch of salt in a saucepan and, while hot, pour it over the chilis. Refrigerate for 30 minutes.

In a bowl, mix the butter with the marmite and spread it on the toasted bread. Serve the hot soup in bowls topped with a slice of bread with marmite butter, some pickled red chilis, and parsley.

1 POUND BEEF SHANK
1 TBSP. FLOUR
SALT
3 ½ TBSP. BUTTER
1 ONION, GRATED
2 CLOVES GARLIC, FINELY CHOPPED
1 TBSP. MARMITE
1 SPRIG OF ROSEMARY
2 SPRIGS OF SAGE
1 BAY LEAF
1 PARSNIP, PEELED AND DICED
   (¾-IN. CUBES)
2 CARROTS, PEELED AND DICED
   (¾-IN. CUBES)
¾ CUP PEARL BARLEY
SALT AND FRESHLY GROUND
   BLACK PEPPER
WORCESTERSHIRE SAUCE

TOPPING
2 FRESH RED CHILIS, SEEDED
   AND SLICED INTO RINGS
3 TBSP. WHITE WINE VINEGAR
1 TBSP. SUGAR
SALT
3 ½ TBSP. BUTTER
2 TSP. MARMITE
4 TO 6 SLICES OF SOURDOUGH BREAD,
   TOASTED
¼ BUNCH OF FLAT-LEAF PARSLEY,
   FINELY CHOPPED

SAOTO

This recipe is enough for about eight bowls, so either make it for a dinner party or freeze any extra. Cut the chicken in half lengthwise (or in large pieces) and fry in a large, deep pan skin-side down in sunflower oil until everything is brown. Remove the chicken from the pan and fry the onions and chopped garlic. Add the two large pieces of galangal and lemongrass, and fry. Return the chicken to the pan and add the chicken stock so everything is submerged. Add the peppercorns, allspice berries, half the celery leaves, the bay leaves, and the Salam leaves. Simmer gently for at least 3 hours. In between, taste to see if the soup is to your liking. Remove the chicken from the pan again, let cool for a moment, and pick the meat into thin strips. Let the stock simmer on low heat until ready to serve (maximum one hour). Before serving, strain the stock over a bowl; what remains in the strainer can be discarded.

While the stock is simmering, make the kecap sauce. In a mortar, grind the four whole garlic cloves and Madame Jeanette chilis into a paste and transfer to a bowl. Crush the last piece of galangal until it is almost completely broken up. In a bowl, mix the sweet and salty kecap together with the garlic-chili mixture. Stir well and add the galangal. You can put this in an empty jam jar and shake to blend. Let the flavors infuse for a few hours. The kecap sauce will keep for 3 months if it's in a clean, airtight jar in the refrigerator.

Add the chicken, rice, bean sprouts, saoto mix, egg, the rest of the celery leaves, and then the hot stock to each bowl. Taste first without the kecap sauce, then add a few tablespoons to taste. For the real go-getter, you can add another Madame Jeanette chili to the bowl.

1 WHOLE CHICKEN (3.5 POUNDS)
3 TBSP. SUNFLOWER OIL
2 LARGE ONIONS, GRATED
5 CLOVES GARLIC, FINELY CHOPPED, PLUS 4 WHOLE CLOVES
2 (1 ½-IN.) PIECES OF GALANGAL, PLUS ONE (1 ¼-IN.) PIECE
2 STALKS OF LEMONGRASS, BRUISED
5 ¼ QUARTS CHICKEN STOCK
2 TBSP. BLACK PEPPERCORNS, COARSELY CRUSHED IN MORTAR
10 ALLSPICE BERRIES

1 LARGE HANDFUL OF CELERY LEAVES, COARSELY CHOPPED
3 BAY LEAVES
5 SALAM LEAVES (OR SUBSTITUTE CURRY LEAVES)
2 MADAME JEANETTE CHILIS (OR SUBSTITUTE LEMON HABANEROS)
14 TBSP. KECAP MANIS (OR SUBSTITUTE SWEET SOY SAUCE)
7 TBSP. KECAP ASIN (OR SUBSTITUTE SOY SAUCE)

TOPPING (PER PERSON)
¼ CUP COOKED WHITE RICE (OPTIONAL)
⅓ CUP MUNG BEAN SPROUTS AND/OR CELERY SLICES
SAOTO MIX (FRIED VERMICELLI, FRIED ONIONS, AND FRIED POTATOES; AVAILABLE ONLINE)
1 HARD-BOILED EGG
1 MADAME JEANETTE CHILI (OR SUBSTITUTE LEMON HABANERO, OPTIONAL)

BLACK BEAN SOUP WITH SALSA AND CRISPY TORTILLA

Finely dice the red onions, garlic, celery, and red bell pepper. Remove the seeds from the chilis and finely chop, keeping the green and red chilis separate. Also finely chop the cilantro, including the stems. In a large pan, heat the olive oil. Reserve a quarter of the cilantro and half of the green chilis. Add the rest of the diced and chopped ingredients to the pan. Finely chop the oregano and add along with the cumin seeds. Briefly sauté everything on high heat, then pour in the black beans, including the liquid. Add the vegetable stock and bay leaf. Let everything boil gently. The soup will slowly thicken. Season with salt and pepper to taste.

To make the topping, mix the tomatoes with the reserved green chilis and cilantro, green onions, lime juice, and a pinch of salt. This is the salsa.

Fry the tortillas in a dry skillet until crispy. Tear or cut into pieces.

Serve the soup in bowls and finish with the salsa and some crispy tortillas. Serve the rest of the crispy tortillas separately.

3 RED ONIONS
3 CLOVES GARLIC
2 CELERY RIBS
1 RED BELL PEPPER
1 GREEN CHILI
1 FRESH RED CHILI
1 BUNCH OF CILANTRO
3 TBSP. OLIVE OIL
½ BUNCH OF OREGANO
1 TSP. CUMIN SEEDS
3 (15-OUNCE) CANS BLACK BEANS
2 CUPS VEGETABLE STOCK
1 BAY LEAF
SALT AND FRESHLY GROUND
   BLACK PEPPER

TOPPING
2 TOMATOES, COARSELY CHOPPED
2 GREEN ONIONS, FINELY CHOPPED
JUICE OF 1 LIME
SALT
4 TO 6 (6-IN.) CORN TORTILLAS

CUTTLEFISH SOUP WITH CROSTINI AND FENNEL SALAD

Cut the cuttlefish into ½-inch strips. Sauté the red onions, garlic, and red chili in a large pan with the olive oil. Add the cuttlefish, along with the ink, diced tomatoes, white wine, bay leaf, basil, and fish stock. Simmer on low heat for 35 minutes. Add the potato and continue to simmer for 10 minutes more. Season to taste with salt and pepper.

Make a small fennel salad for the topping. Chop the fennel as finely as you can. Season with the olive oil, basil, lemon zest, and lemon juice. Make some crostini from stale bread by brushing the slices with olive oil and placing them briefly in a grill pan or under the oven broiler until crispy on both sides.

Divide the soup among deep plates and finish with some fennel salad and crostini.

1 ½ POUNDS CLEANED CUTTLEFISH, THAWED IF FROZEN
2 RED ONIONS, GRATED
4 CLOVES GARLIC, FINELY CHOPPED
½ FRESH RED CHILI, FINELY CHOPPED
5 TBSP. OLIVE OIL
2 ½ (1-OUNCE) PACKETS OF SQUID INK (AVAILABLE ONLINE)
1 (14-OUNCE) CAN DICED TOMATOES
⅔ CUP WHITE WINE
1 BAY LEAF
5 TO 7 BASIL LEAVES, FINELY CHOPPED
3 CUPS FISH STOCK OR WATER
7 OUNCES POTATO, PEELED AND DICED (⅜-IN. CUBES)
SALT AND FRESHLY GROUND BLACK PEPPER

TOPPING
1 FENNEL BULB
2 TBSP. OLIVE OIL, PLUS MORE AS NEEDED
½ BUNCH OF BASIL, FINELY CHOPPED
GRATED ZEST AND JUICE OF 1 ORGANIC LEMON
4 TO 6 SLICES OF HEARTY (SOURDOUGH) BREAD, SLIGHTLY STALE

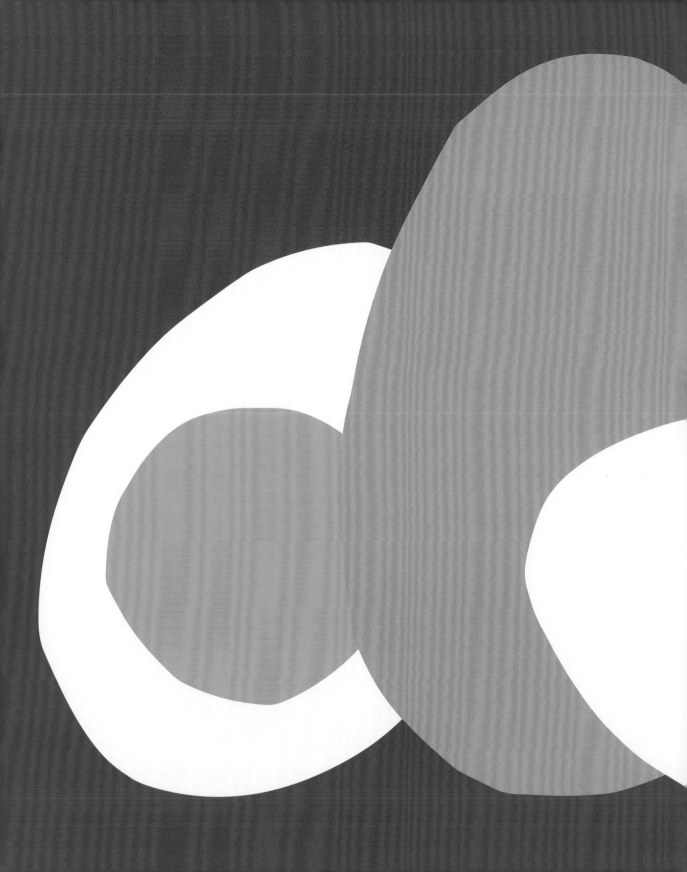

CABBAGE BROTH

WITH PALM CABBAGE AND A FRIED EGG

Cut the pointed cabbage and onions lengthwise into quarters. Roast them on a grill until they have substantial black spots. Put a large pan over medium-high heat containing the dried shiitake, lemon juice, soy sauce, and 4 ¼ cups of water. Bring to a boil and simmer for 30 minutes. Let cool and refrigerate overnight. The next day, strain the contents of the pan through a cheesecloth and drain so that a clear stock remains.

To make the topping, cut the large veins from the palm cabbage leaves and discard them. Bring a pan with 4 cups of water to a boil and add the salt. Cook the palm cabbage for 5 minutes until tender. Then, transfer the palm cabbage into ice water so that it does not cook through and the beautiful color is preserved. Drain the palm cabbage and cut into coarse pieces about 1 ¼ inches wide. In a skillet, melt 3 ½ tablespoons of the butter. Add the garlic and palm cabbage. Cook, stirring, for 2 minutes and set aside.

Warm up the stock.

Heat a second large skillet over medium-high heat with the remaining 3 ½ tablespoons of butter in it. Tap a slit in an egg with the side of a knife. Break open over the skillet and gently slide the egg into the pan so that the yolk does not break. Repeat with the rest of the eggs, trying not to put them too close together. When the egg whites have solidified, they are ready. Sprinkle them with salt and pepper, if necessary. Place a coffee cup or glass over each fried egg and cut out a neat, round egg. Do this for each egg and lift them out of the pan with a spatula. Place each egg in a deep plate, divide the palm cabbage leaves among the plates, and pour the hot stock around them.

1 LARGE POINTED (SWEETHEART)
  CABBAGE (OR SUBSTITUTE
  A SAVOY CABBAGE)
2 ONIONS
¾ CUP DRIED SHIITAKE MUSHROOMS
JUICE OF 2 LEMONS
6 ½ TBSP. SOY SAUCE

TOPPING
12 YOUNG PALM CABBAGE LEAVES
1 TBSP. SALT, PLUS SOME EXTRA
7 TBSP. BUTTER
1 CLOVE GARLIC, CRUSHED
4 TO 6 EGGS
FRESHLY GROUND BLACK PEPPER
  (OPTIONAL)

RAWON SOUP
WITH GREEN ONION AND BEAN SPROUTS

In a mortar or food processor, grind the chili, nuts, ginger, makrut leaves, galangal, coriander, turmeric, trassi, kecap manis, onions, and salt until you have a curry paste. Sauté the curry paste in a large pan with the sunflower oil until oil starts to separate. Add the meat and fry briefly until the liquid runs out. Add the tamarind water and simmer until (almost) boiled dry. Top up with 11 cups of water (or until everything is submerged) and cook along with the lemongrass until the meat is tender. This takes 2 to 3 hours. If it gets too dry, add more water to the pan.

Pick the meat off the bone and add (with or without bone) to the pan. Pour the rawon soup into bowls and garnish with the green onion, bean sprouts, cilantro leaves, lime wedges, and chili oil.

1 RED LOMBOK CHILI, SEEDED (OR SUBSTITUTE RED FRESNO OR CAYENNE)

2 KLUWAK NUTS, SOAKED IN LUKEWARM WATER FOR AT LEAST 15 MINUTES

2 ½ TBSP. PEELED AND GRATED GINGER

3 MAKRUT LIME LEAVES, VEINS REMOVED AND VERY THINLY CUT

1 PIECE GALANGAL (ABOUT THE SIZE OF THE TIP OF YOUR THUMB), PEELED, STEM REMOVED, AND FINELY CHOPPED

½ TSP. CORIANDER SEEDS

1 (1 ¼-IN.) PIECE TURMERIC ROOT, PEELED AND FINELY CHOPPED

1 TSP. TRASSI (FERMENTED SHRIMP PASTE) OR MISO

2 TO 3 TBSP. KECAP MANIS (OR SUBSTITUTE SWEET SOY SAUCE)

5 RED ONIONS, GRATED

2 WHITE ONIONS, GRATED

SALT

2 TBSP. SUNFLOWER OIL

1 ⅓ POUNDS BONE-IN BEEF SHANK

1 TBSP. TAMARIND WATER

1 STALK OF LEMONGRASS, THE INNER PART FINELY CHOPPED

TOPPING
3 GREEN ONIONS, FINELY CHOPPED
1 CUP MUNG BEAN SPROUTS
½ BUNCH OF CILANTRO, LEAVES ONLY
4 TO 6 LIME WEDGES
CHILI OIL

TRUFFLE SOUP

WITH PUFF PASTRY LID

This recipe makes about 6 bowls because it would be wasteful to prepare a small batch with these ingredients. Use it for a dinner party or freeze the extra.

In a large saucepan, submerge the veal shank in about 5 quarts of cold water. Slowly bring to a boil and simmer for 6 hours. If too much water evaporates, you can add more cold water.

Cut the carrot, leek, onion, and garlic in half lengthwise. After the 6 hours, add the vegetables, bay leaf, and peppercorns. Let the vegetables cook for 1 hour and then scoop them out of the stock with the shank. Strain the stock over a pan through a wet, clean cheesecloth. Pick the meat from the shank and cut into small cubes.

Preheat the oven to 350°F. Divide the cubed meat, with the small, cubed vegetables, truffle, and foie gras among ovenproof soup bowls and pour in some of the Noilly Prat. Fill the ovenproof bowls two-thirds full with the veal stock. Brush the edges of the bowls with a little egg yolk and place the puff pastry slices on top. Press gently along the edges to seal. Brush the puff pastry with a little egg yolk as well. Bake for 17 minutes in the hot oven.

4 ½ POUNDS VEAL SHANK
1 LARGE CARROT
1 LARGE LEEK
1 LARGE WHITE ONION
1 BULB GARLIC, EXCESS
   PEELS REMOVED
1 BAY LEAF
10 BLACK PEPPERCORNS

TOPPING
1 SMALL CARROT, IN SMALL CUBES
1 LEEK, IN SMALL CUBES
2 SALAD TURNIPS, IN SMALL CUBES
1 TRUFFLE (AS MUCH AS YOU'RE
   WILLING TO PAY FOR), THINLY
   SLICED
1 OUNCE FOIE GRAS PER PERSON,
   DICED
3 TBSP. NOILLY PRAT OR OTHER
   DRY VERMOUTH
1 EGG YOLK, BEATEN
6 CIRCLES OF PUFF PASTRY, CUT 1 IN.
   LARGER IN DIAMETER THAN
   THE SOUP BOWLS

146

INDEX BY SOUP TYPE

BY INGREDIENT

BREADCRUMBS
Tomato Cream Soup with Sausage
or Meatballs 72

BROCCOLI
Green Curry Soup with Broccoli 108

BURRATA
Green Gazpacho with Burrata 100
Peach Soup with Burrata 66

CABBAGE
Borscht 94
Cabbage Broth with Palm Cabbage
and a Fried Egg 142
Caldo Verde with Chorizo 110
Red Cabbage Soup with Ricotta
Dumplings 88

CARROT
Beef and Vegetable Soup 128
Borscht 94
Brown Windsor 130
Carrot and Coriander Soup 60
Chicken Soup 120
Fish Stock 21
Meat Stock 22
Roasted Vitelotte Potato Soup with
Goat Cheese 92
Truffle Soup with Puff Pastry Lid 146
Vegetable Stock 21
Yellow Pea Soup 50

CASSAVA
Sweet Potato Soup with Cassava
and Plantain 62

CAULIFLOWER
Beef and Vegetable Soup 128
Tomato Cream Soup with Sausage
or Meatballs 72

CELERIAC
Dutch Split Pea Soup 102
Meat Stock 22
Mussel Chowder with Saffron 40
Mussel Stock 40
Tomato Cream Soup with Sausage
or Meatballs 72

CELERY
Black Bean Soup with Salsa and
Crispy Tortilla 136
Borscht 94

Carrot and Coriander Soup 60
Chicken Soup 120
Chicken Stock 21
Cold Beet Soup with Purple Basil
and Blackberries 90
Fish Stock 21
Meat Stock 22
Mussel Chowder with Saffron 40
Mussel Stock 40
North Sea Fish Soup 76
Peach Soup with Burrata 66
Purple Sweet Potato Soup 96
Red Cabbage Soup with Ricotta
Dumplings 88
Saoto 132
Shrimp Bisque 68
Surinamese Brown Bean Soup 124
Tomato Cream Soup with Sausage
or Meatballs 72
Vegetable Stock 21
Watercress Soup 112
Yellow Pea Soup 50
Zucchini and Bread Soup 106
Zuppa di Baccalà 84

CELERY LEAVES
Beef and Vegetable Soup 128
Chicken Soup 120
Chicken Stock 21
Dutch Split Pea Soup 102
Meat Stock 22
Peanut Soup 122
Saoto 132
Surinamese Brown Bean Soup 124
Yellow Pea Soup 50

CHERRY
Cold Beet Soup with Purple Basil
and Blackberries 90

CHERVIL
Sunflower Seed and Celeriac Soup
with Parsnip and Sage 36

CHICKEN
Chicken Soup 120
Chicken Stock 21
Peanut Soup 122
Saoto 132
Surinamese Brown Bean Soup 124

CHICKPEA
Harira 80

CHILI OIL
Corn and Jalapeño Soup 42
Green Curry Soup with Broccoli 108
Laksa 44
Rawon Soup with Green Onion and
Bean Sprouts 144
Thai Coconut Soup 28

CHILI PEPPER
Black Bean Soup with Salsa and
Crispy Tortilla 136
Brown Windsor 130
Cold Beet Soup with Purple Basil
and Blackberries 90
Corn and Jalapeño Soup 42
Cuttlefish Soup with Crostini and
Fennel Salad 138
Dahl 48
Fennel and White Bean Soup 34
Goulash with Bell Peppers 74
Green Curry Soup with Broccoli
108
Green Gazpacho with Burrata 100
Laksa 44
Lentil and Pumpkin Soup 58
Noodles in Beef Broth 82
North Sea Fish Soup 76
Peach Soup with Burrata 66
Purple Sweet Potato Soup 96
Rawon Soup with Green Onion and
Bean Sprouts 144
Saoto 132
Surinamese Brown Bean Soup 124
Sweet-and-Sour Shells with
Turmeric 64
Yellow Gazpacho 52

CHIPOTLE HOT SAUCE
Carrot and Coriander Soup 60

CHIVES
Vichyssoise with Potato Crumble 46

CINNAMON STICK
Harira 80
Noodles in Beef Broth 82

COCONUT FLAKES
Green Curry Soup with Broccoli 108
Sunflower Seed and Celeriac Soup
with Parsnip and Sage 36
Sweet Potato Soup with Cassava
and Plantain 62

COCONUT MILK AND CREAM
Green Curry Soup with Broccoli 108
Laksa 44
Peanut Soup 122
Pumpkin Soup with Ginger and
    Coconut 56
Purple Sweet Potato Soup 96
Thai Coconut Soup 28
Yellow Pea Soup 50

COGNAC
Shellfish Stock 22
Shrimp Bisque 68

COLATURA DI ALICI
North Sea Fish Soup 76

CORIANDER
Black Bean Soup with Salsa and
    Crispy Tortilla 136
Carrot and Coriander Soup 60
Dahl 48
Green Curry Soup with Broccoli 108
Green Gazpacho with Burrata 100
Harira 80
Laksa 44
Purple Sweet Potato Soup 96
Rawon Soup with Green Onion and
    Bean Sprouts 144
Sweet-and-Sour Shells with
    Turmeric 64
Sweet Potato Soup with Cassava
    and Plantain 62
Thai Coconut Soup 28
Yellow Gazpacho 52

CORN
Corn and Jalapeño Soup 42
Yellow Gazpacho 52

CREAM
Green Asparagus and Pea Soup
    with a Salad of Haricots Verts
    and Almonds 104
Jerusalem Artichoke and Hazelnut
    Soup with Watercress Salad 30
Mushroom Cream Soup with
    Parmesan Croutons 126
Mussel Chowder with Saffron 40
Parsley and Wild Garlic Soup with
    Snails 114
Tomato Cream Soup with Sausage
    or Meatballs 72
White Asparagus Soup with

Tarragon Dressing 32

CRÈME FRAICHE
Borscht 94
Cold Beet Soup with Purple Basil
    and Blackberries 90
Mushroom Cream Soup with
    Parmesan Croutons 126
Pumpkin Soup with Ginger and
    Coconut 56
Watercress Soup 112

CUCUMBER
Green Gazpacho with Burrata 100
Peach Soup with Burrata 66
Yellow Gazpacho 52

DILL
Borscht 94

DOUBANJIANG
Noodles in Beef Broth 82

EGG
Cabbage Broth with Palm Cabbage
    and a Fried Egg 142
Red Cabbage Soup with Ricotta
    Dumplings 88
Saoto 132

EGGPLANT
Green Curry Soup with Broccoli
    108

ENOKI
Mushroom Stock 22

FENNEL
Cuttlefish Soup with Crostini and
    Fennel Salad 138
Fennel and White Bean Soup 34
North Sea Fish Soup 76
Shellfish Stock 22
Shrimp Bisque 68
Tomato Cream Soup with Sausage
    or Meatballs 72

FISH
Cold Beet Soup with Purple Basil
    and Blackberries 90
Cuttlefish Soup with Crostini and
    Fennel Salad 138
Fish Stock 21
North Sea Fish Soup 76

Zuppa di Baccalà 84

FISH SAUCE
Laksa 44
North Sea Fish Soup 76
Sweet-and-Sour Shells with
    Turmeric 64
Thai Coconut Soup 28

FOIE GRAS
Truffle Soup with Puff Pastry Lid
    146

GALANGAL
Green Curry Soup with Broccoli
    108
Rawon Soup with Green Onion and
    Bean Sprouts 144
Saoto 132
Thai Coconut Soup 28

GHEE
Lentil and Pumpkin Soup 58

GINGER
Dahl 48
Green Gazpacho with Burrata 100
Laksa 44
Noodles in Beef Broth 82
Peanut Soup 122
Pumpkin Soup with Ginger and
    Coconut 56
Purple Sweet Potato Soup 96
Rawon Soup with Green Onion and
    Bean Sprouts 144
Sweet-and-Sour Shells with
    Turmeric 64
Thai Coconut Soup 28
Yellow Gazpacho 52

GOAT CHEESE
Roasted Vitelotte Potato Soup with
    Goat Cheese 92

GRAPES
Ajo Blanco (White Gazpacho) with
    Grapes and Toasted Almond 26

GREEN ONION
Black Bean Soup with Salsa and
    Crispy Tortilla 136
Laksa 44
Noodles in Beef Broth 82

Rawon Soup with Green Onion
and Bean Sprouts 144
Sweet-and-Sour Shells with
Turmeric 64
Thai Coconut Soup 28

GRISSINI
Pumpkin Soup with Ginger and
Coconut 56

GRUYÈRE
Onion Soup 118

HAZELNUT, HAZELNUT OIL
Jerusalem Artichoke and Hazelnut
Soup with Watercress Salad 30

HORSERADISH
Vichyssoise with Potato Crumble
46
Watercress Soup 112

JERUSALEM ARTICHOKE
Jerusalem Artichoke and Hazelnut
Soup with Watercress Salad 30

KATJANG PEDIS
Yellow Pea Soup 50

KETJAP
Peanut Soup 122
Rawon Soup with Green Onion
and Bean Sprouts 144
Saoto 132

KLUWAK NUTS
Rawon Soup with Green Onion
and Bean Sprouts 144

KOHLRABI
Borscht 94

KOMBU SHEET
Dashi 22
Mushroom Stock 22

LAMB
Meat Stock 22

LEEK
Beef and Vegetable Soup 128
Borscht 94
Carrot and Coriander Soup 60
Chicken Soup 120

Chicken Stock 21
Dutch Split Pea Soup 102
Meat Stock 22
Mussel Chowder with Saffron 40
North Sea Fish Soup 76
Roasted Vitelotte Potato Soup with
Goat Cheese 92
Shrimp Bisque 68
Truffle Soup with Puff Pastry Lid
146
Vegetable Stock 21
Vichyssoise with Potato Crumble 46

LEMON GRASS
Green Curry Soup with Broccoli
108
Laksa 44
Peanut Soup 122
Rawon Soup with Green Onion
and Bean Sprouts 144
Saoto 132
Sweet-and-Sour Shells with
Turmeric 64
Thai Coconut Soup 28
Yellow Pea Soup 50

LENTILS
Harira 80
Lentil and Pumpkin Soup 58

LIME
Black Bean Soup with Salsa and
Crispy Tortilla 136
Dahl 48
Green Curry Soup with Broccoli
108
Laksa 44
Lentil and Pumpkin Soup 58
Peanut Soup 122
Rawon Soup with Green Onion
and Bean Sprouts 144
Sweet-and-Sour Shells with
Turmeric 64
Sweet Potato Soup with Cassava
and Plantain 62
Thai Coconut Soup 28

LIME LEAF
Green Curry Soup with Broccoli
108
Laksa 44
Peanut Soup 122
Rawon Soup with Green Onion
and Bean Sprouts 144

Sweet-and-Sour Shells with
Turmeric 64
Thai Coconut Soup 28

LOVAGE
Vegetable Stock 21

MACE
Beef and Vegetable Soup 128
Chicken Soup 120

MANGO
Yellow Gazpacho 52

MARJORAM
Goulash with Bell Peppers 74

MARMITE
Brown Windsor 130

MASCARPONE
Tomato Cream Soup with Sausage
or Meatballs 72

MINT
Green Gazpacho with Burrata 100
Yellow Gazpacho 52

MISO
Sunflower Seed and Celeriac Soup
with Parsnip and Sage 36

MUSHROOM
Chicken Soup 120
Green Curry Soup with Broccoli
108
Mushroom Cream Soup with
Parmesan Croutons 126
Mushroom Stock 22
Thai Coconut Soup 28

NAAN
Dahl 48

NOILLY PRAT
North Sea Fish Soup 76
Parsley and Wild Garlic Soup with
Snails 114
Truffle Soup with Puff Pastry
Lid 146

156

SAGE
Brown Windsor 130
Sunflower Seed and Celeriac Soup
with Parsnip and Sage 36

SALAM LEAF
Saoto 132

SALT PORK
Surinamese Brown Bean Soup 124
Yellow Pea Soup 50

SAMBAL
Peanut Soup 122
Surinamese Brown Bean Soup 124
Yellow Pea Soup 50

SAMPHIRE
Shrimp Bisque 68

SEA LAVENDER
Shrimp Bisque 68

SHALLOT
Borscht 94
Chicken Stock 21
Fennel and White Bean Soup 34
Green Curry Soup with Broccoli 108
Laksa 44
North Sea Fish Soup 76
Sunflower Seed and Celeriac Soup
with Parsnip and Sage 36
Yellow Pea Soup 50

SHAOXING RICE WINE
Noodles in Beef Broth 82

SHELLFISH
Laksa 44
Mussel Chowder with Saffron 40
Mussel Stock 40
Shellfish Stock 22
Shrimp Bisque 68
Sweet-and-Sour Shells with
Turmeric 64
Watercress Soup 112

SHIITAKE
Cabbage Broth with Palm Cabbage
and a Fried Egg 142
Dashi 22
Mushroom Stock 22

SMEN
Harira 80

SNAILS
Parsley and Wild Garlic Soup with
Snails 114

SOUR CREAM
Goulash with Bell Peppers 74
Sweet Potato Soup with Cassava
and Plantain 62

SOY SAUCE
Cabbage Broth with Palm Cabbage
and a Fried Egg 142
Dashi 22
Mushroom Cream Soup with
Parmesan Croutons 126
Noodles in Beef Broth 82

SPINACH
Dahl 48
Green Asparagus and Pea Soup
with a Salad of Haricots Verts
and Almonds 104
Green Curry Soup with Broccoli 108
Green Gazpacho with Burrata 100
North Sea Fish Soup 76

SPLIT PEA
Dahl 48
Dutch Split Pea Soup 102
Yellow Pea Soup 50

STAR ANISE
Noodles in Beef Broth 82

SUNFLOWER SEEDS
Sunflower Seed and Celeriac Soup
with Parsnip and Sage 36

SWEET POTATO
Purple Sweet Potato Soup 96
Sweet Potato Soup with Cassava
and Plantain 62

TAMARIND WATER
Rawon Soup with Green Onion and
Bean Sprouts 144

TARRAGON
North Sea Fish Soup 76
Peach Soup with Burrata 66
White Asparagus Soup with
Tarragon Dressing 32

THYME
Borscht 94
Chicken Stock 21
Fennel and White Bean Soup 34
Green Asparagus and Pea Soup
with a Salad of Haricots Verts
and Almonds 104
Jerusalem Artichoke and Hazelnut
Soup with Watercress Salad 30
Meat Stock 22
Mussel Chowder with Saffron 40
Mussel Stock 40
North Sea Fish Soup 76
Onion Soup 118
Parsley and Wild Garlic Soup with
Snails 114
Red Cabbage Soup with Ricotta
Dumplings 88
Shrimp Bisque 68
Vegetable Stock 21
Vichyssoise with Potato Crumble 46
Zucchini and Bread Soup 106

TOMATO, TOMATO PASTE
Black Bean Soup with Salsa and
Crispy Tortilla 136
Chicken Soup 120
Cuttlefish Soup with Crostini and
Fennel Salad 138
Dahl 48
Goulash with Bell Peppers 74
Green Gazpacho with Burrata 100
Harira 80
Lentil and Pumpkin Soup 58
Noodles in Beef Broth 82
North Sea Fish Soup 76
Purple Sweet Potato Soup 96
Shellfish Stock 22
Shrimp Bisque 68
Surinamese Brown Bean Soup 124
Sweet-and-Sour Shells with
Turmeric 64
Tomato Cream Soup with Sausage
or Meatballs 72
Yellow Gazpacho 52
Zuppa di Baccalà 84

TOM YUM PASTE
Thai Coconut Soup **28**

TORTILLA
Black Bean Soup with Salsa and
    Crispy Tortilla **136**

TRASSI
Rawon Soup with Green Onion and
    Bean Sprouts **144**

TRUFFLE
Truffle Soup with Puff Pastry Lid **146**

VITELOTTE POTATO
Roasted Vitelotte Potato Soup with
    Goat Cheese **92**

WATERCRESS
Jerusalem Artichoke and Hazelnut
    Soup with Watercress Salad **30**
Watercress Soup **112**

WILD GARLIC
Parsley and Wild Garlic Soup with
    Snails **114**

WINE
see also cognac, Pernod, port,
    Ricard, Shaoxing rice wine
Cuttlefish Soup with Crostini and
    Fennel Salad **138**
Fish Stock **21**
Meat Stock **22**
Mussel Chowder with Saffron **40**
Mussel Stock **40**
Shellfish Stock **22**
Shrimp Bisque **68**

YARDLONG BEAN
Peanut Soup **122**

YOGURT
Carrot and Coriander Soup **60**
Dahl **48**

YUZU JUICE
Dashi **22**

ZUCCHINI
Parsley and Wild Garlic Soup with
    Snails **114**
Zucchini and Bread Soup **106**

CREDITS

GOOD SOUP: 52 COLORFUL RECIPES FOR YEAR-ROUND COMFORT

AUTHORS
JORIS BIJDENDIJK AND SAMUEL LEVIE

TRANSLATOR
BART LEVER, COURTESY OF ERIKSEN TRANSLATIONS

RECIPE ADAPTATIONS
ANDREA CHESMAN, COURTESY OF ERIKSEN TRANSLATIONS

U.S. EDITION PUBLISHER & CREATIVE DIRECTOR
ILONA OPPENHEIM

U.S. EDITION EDITOR
KARA PICKMAN, PICKMAN EDITORIAL

U.S. EDITION EDITORIAL COORDINATOR
JESSICA FAROY

U.S. EDITION PROOFREADER
ILEANA OROZA

COVER DESIGN & LAYOUT
DUTCH EDITION: WE ARE OUT OF OFFICE & SACHA VAN DEN HAK
U.S. EDITION: JEFFERSON QUINTANA

PRINTER
PRINTED AND BOUND IN CHINA BY
SHENZHEN RELIANCE PRINTERS

GOOD SOUP: 52 COLORFUL RECIPES FOR YEAR-ROUND COMFORT
FIRST PUBLISHED IN THE UNITED STATES BY TRA PUBLISHING
2023. TEXT AND RECIPES COPYRIGHT © 2022 BY JORIS BIJDENDIJK
AND SAMUEL LEVIE. PHOTOGRAPHY COPYRIGHT © 2022 BY
SASKIA VAN OSNABRUGGE. ORIGINAL TITLE: *SOEP VAN SAM EN
JORIS.* FIRST PUBLISHED IN 2022 BY NIJGH CUISINE, AMSTERDAM.

ISBN: 979-8-9866406-6-2

GOOD SOUP: 52 COLORFUL RECIPES FOR YEAR-ROUND COMFORT
IS PRINTED ON FOREST STEWARDSHIP COUNCIL-CERTIFIED PAPER
FROM WELL-MANAGED FORESTS. TRA PUBLISHING IS COMMITTED
TO SUSTAINABILITY IN ITS MATERIALS AND PRACTICES.

FSC
www.fsc.org
MIX
Paper from
responsible sources
FSC® C102842

TRA PUBLISHING
245 NE 37TH STREET
MIAMI, FL 33137
TRAPUBLISHING.COM

tra.publishing

2 3 4 5 6 7 8 9 10